HOW TO RECRUIT

To Tracey and Michael

How to Recruit

Iain Maitland

Gower

Published by
Gower Publishing Company Limited
Gower House
Croft Road
Aldershot
Hants GU11 3HR
England

Gower Publishing Company
Old Post Road
Brookfield
Vermont 05036
USA

British Library Cataloguing Data
  Maitland, Iain
    How to recruit.
    1. Recruitment
    I. Title
    658.311

ISBN 0–566–02968–5

Printed in Great Britain by
Billing & Sons Ltd, Worcester

Other books by the same author

The Barclays Guide to Managing Staff for the Small Business
(Basil Blackwell)
How to Win at Job Hunting (Business Books)
How to Win at Interviews (Business Books)
How to Buy and Run a Shop (Northcote House)
Franchising (Mercury)
Running a Successful Advertising Campaign (Telegraph Publications)
The Secrets of Successful Business Plans (Heinemann)

Contents

List of figures

Preface

Recruiting the right person for a job is a time-consuming and lengthy process. It need not be difficult though, so long as it is approached in a careful and systematic manner.

Recruitment must start with a thorough assessment of immediate staff requirements. The vacant job should be analysed, and a job description and employee specification written out to show what the job involves and the type of person who is needed to do it. Attention must also be given to future staff requirements, with any prospective employee able enough to be transferred or promoted to other jobs as they arise.

Next, a pool of suitable people has to be found and sufficiently attracted to want to apply for the job. Possible sources of recruitment – internal and external – have to be studied and selected. Informative and appealing advertisements need to be designed. Both sources of recruitment and advertisements ought to be monitored to ensure that they reach and interest the appropriate people.

Applicants must then be screened – by letter, curriculum vitae, telephone or application form – and reduced to a shortlist of candidates to be interviewed and tested for the job. The most suitable candidate should be chosen and an offer of employment made. If that is accepted, the remaining candidates ought to be rejected.

A successful recruitment policy should continue with the new employee being helped to settle into the job as quickly and smoothly as possible. He or she must be regularly appraised to see that standards of work rate and performance are maintained. The entire recruitment process should then be reviewed, and changes and improvements implemented as necessary.

This book – which is written for all business owners and managers responsible for recruiting their own staff – is divided into eight chapters, each dealing with a separate stage of recruitment on a step-by-step basis. At the end of every chapter, a short series of questions and answers acts as both a checklist and summary of key points.

Throughout the text, examples of recruitment documents – such as job descriptions, application forms and staff appraisal forms – are reproduced to illustrate the information given. Many of these examples have been supplied by some of the UK's leading companies, highlighting how they approach staff recruitment and selection.

Avoiding discrimination – on the grounds of sex, marital status, race and disability – is a theme referred to throughout the text. It is reflected also in the appendices, where the main legislative acts and codes of good practice are summarized. Detailed lists of helpful organizations and useful books are included there as well.

Despite stressing the importance of adopting a non-discriminatory attitude, I have used the pronouns 'he' and 'him' in preference to 'he or she' and 'him or her'. This should be regarded as a (non-sexist) shorthand version which is far less tedious to write and read.

To learn all about how to recruit staff, read on . . .

Iain Maitland

Acknowledgements

I wish to thank the following individuals for their kind assistance. Acknowledgements are also due to their companies for generously allowing me to reproduce their documents within this book:

- Stephanie Bassett
  The Equal Opportunities Commission
- Chris Cooper
  Halifax Building Society
- Alison Davis
  Turret Group Plc
- Robert Feltham
  NFER-Nelson Ltd
- Mollie Fox
  Banham Zoo Ltd
- Jessica Grierson
  Pentos Retailing Group Ltd
- Joan Harding
  The Boots Company Plc
- Neil Hubbard
  Oracle Teletext Ltd

- Edison Kangalee
  The Commission for Racial Equality
- Bob Knights
  Royal Mail
- Norman Lloyd
  Suffolk Group Radio Plc
- Michael Moore
  Express Newspapers Plc
- Paula Ryder
  Betty's Café Tea Rooms Ltd
- Trevor White
  East Anglian Daily Times Company Ltd
- Michelle Woodliff
  Selfridges Ltd
- Michael Wright
  The Department of Employment Group

Thanks to Steve Palmer at the Institute of Personnel Management and to The Personnel Department at London Zoo as well.

Finally, my special thanks to Malcolm Stern for his endless patience and to Tracey for her constant help.

IM

xiii

1   Planning staff requirements

The recruitment process begins when an employee is to be transferred or promoted to another post, notice of resignation or dismissal is given or retirement is planned. You must start by assessing your immediate staff needs, deciding whether the job needs changing and what sort of person you wish to recruit. A thorough analysis of the job has to be carried out, following which a job description and an employee specification – detailing the work and the type of person required to do it – ought to be drawn up. You should consider the future staff needs of your company, taking on employees who are capable of moving into other positions as necessary.

Studying immediate needs

When a vacancy occurs, the manager responsible for filling it typically assumes that the job should remain exactly as it is. Furthermore, he simply looks around – whether internally or externally – for a new employee who is a carbon copy of the one who is leaving. He just wants everything to proceed as it has done, with minimal fuss and inconvenience to him.

Such an automatic response is unwise. The job may need updating in some way. Its role might not complement – and could even clash with – the aims and objectives of other jobs. Duties allocated to the employee may overlap with those of his colleagues (and could possibly be done better by them). Responsibilities might have been ignored and left to fellow employees to attend to.

Perhaps the hours of employment ought also to be adjusted. A full-time employee may not have sufficient work to keep him totally occupied. It could be more sensible to streamline the job on a part-time basis, bringing in staff to cover only the busiest hours or days of the week. It might even be possible – especially if some tasks or responsibilities are to be given to others – to continue the job on a temporary basis, with short-term appointments being made when needed.

Clearly, the results of leaving a (unsatisfactory) job unchanged could be detrimental to both the department and the company itself. If roles and duties are duplicated – far from uncommon in large companies – disruptive tensions may arise between employees competing for the same work. Should responsibilities be forced upon others, resentment and ill feeling could develop. Employing an underworked employee leads to an unnecessarily high wage bill.

Seeking to recruit an exact replica of the departing employee is illogical. He may not be ideally suited to the job as it is now (and would be even less suitable if it is to be amended). Should he have been in that position for some time, he will probably have moulded the work to suit his own particular strengths, dropping or passing on those tasks that might illuminate his weaknesses. Even if he were the perfect employee, finding a precise replacement – with identical skills, work experience and so on – is impossible.

The consequences of employing an unsuitable person for the job can be severe. The new employee's work performance may be poor as he – possibly like his predecessor – is unable to handle all of the demands on him. His work rate and morale could subsequently fall with conflicts occurring amongst fellow staff whom he lets down or who have to cover for him. Eventually, after the costs of recruitment, training, pay and fringe benefits, administration and supervision have been incurred (for little in return), he will resign or have to be dismissed. The recruitment process then has to begin all over again (and repeated until the manager finally approaches the task correctly).

The creation of a job vacancy – whatever the type and level of job – must not be seen a chore to be dealt with as quickly as possible. It should be regarded as an opportunity to stand back and comprehensively assess the job and the type of employee wanted. Only then can recruitment truly begin and proceed to a successful conclusion.

Analysing the job

Job analysis – the process of assembling and studying information relating to all aspects of a particular post – will enable you to make the correct decision about its future. If it is to continue in some form, you will further be able to deduce the type of person needed to do it successfully.

A complete and thorough analysis of the job ought to reveal the fullest possible details about:

- its purpose
- its position
- its main duties
- the qualities required
- the work environment.

Purpose

Initially, you must identify exactly the main aims and objectives of the job. Jot down what the employee is expected to achieve within his department and company. Then assess whether these targets are actually being met. If not, changes ought to be made.

Position

The job title, its location, those to whom the employee is answerable and for whom he is responsible ought to be recorded. A note should also be made about the colleagues he works alongside, other employees and departments he comes into contact with on a (semi-) regular basis and any opportunities for future transfer and promotion. A simple organization chart, highlighting the position of the job, may be useful. Inspecting this chart could help you to decide if you wish to reorganize your department, improving chains of command and communication.

Main duties

A list of key tasks must be written out along with any procedures which have to be followed, standards that need to be reached and maintained and methods of measuring, assessing and recording them. Consider which tasks are easy and hard to do, agreeable and disagreeable and so on. Think also about the limits of the employee's authority and responsibilities. Assuming all duties are being carried out as anticipated – and if not, adjustments will need to be made –

you then have to consider which should remain, be dropped, re-assigned to others and so forth.

The qualities required

Taking each of the main tasks in turn, it is sensible to contemplate carefully what specific qualities are required if they are all to be done well. Note them down under the general headings of skills, knowledge and experience. If – or when – you start seeking a new employee, you'll be looking for all these qualities in the successful candidate.

The work environment

Study the physical and social environment in which the work is carried out. This is the backdrop against which the job takes place. Not surprisingly, it will thus influence both the quality and quantity of work done. You may feel that it's time for various amendments and alternatives to be implemented.

All these details – which are absolutely essential if you are to decide upon the job's future and the person required to do it properly – should be relatively easy to collate. You'll probably already be aware of much that you need to know through having observed the existing employee doing the job on a day-to-day basis. You may even have done the job yourself in the past. However, there are additional sources of assistance which should be approached so you can build up a comprehensive and accurate picture of the job.

You can interview the employee who is leaving, all his colleagues and his immediate superior. Ask them to describe and talk about different aspects of the job (its purpose, position, and so on), thus confirming or invalidating your existing information, filling in gaps and developing your overall knowledge. A simple questionnaire – to make certain that all main areas are discussed – may be helpful, with such questions as: which employees do you work with every day? what other departments do you deal with? and so on.

Those employees in the same or similar employment can be asked to keep a work diary. They carefully record their daily activities, noting how often various tasks were done, the way in which they were completed, and monitored by the company and so forth. Clearly, these will provide an authoritative, factual basis for subsequent analysis.

You should also study any other documentary evidence that may be available. Perhaps the job was analysed before and detailed notes were filed away for future reference. Records may – indeed should – have been kept for staff appraisal, disciplinary, grievance and exit interviews. These will be worth checking, possibly supplying useful background data of some use to you. (See Appraising the new employee, page 158.)

Once you have written out your extensive notes and are convinced you know everything there is to know, you can reach a decision about the job. Assuming it is to continue – typically with some amendments and updating – you should then move on with the recruitment process by transferring the key details of the notes to a job description and employee specification. (See Drafting a job description, as follows, and Drawing up an employee specification, page 12.)

Examples of job descriptions and employee specifications – showing the type of information gathered up during the job analysis – are given as Figures 1.1–1.3 later in the chapter.

Drafting a job description

A job description, detailing the main purpose, duties and responsibilities of a job, can be drawn up from the information obtained during the job analysis. It has many practical uses. So far as recruitment is concerned, it will help you to decide upon the exact skills, knowledge and experience needed to do the job well. It can also provide the facts required for job advertisements and influence the structure and contents of application forms. Then it can be sent to job applicants thus enabling them to assess whether this is the type of work they want to do. If not, it will save you the time and expense involved in dealing with their applications and possibly interviewing them.

When pre-screening applicants, you can compare previous work experience referred to in application forms, letters and curricula vitae with those tasks that make up this particular job. During interviews, you will find it useful to refer to when you have to talk or answer questions about the job. Tests, especially those that place candidates in simulated work situations, can also be developed from a job description.

Following recruitment, the job description may be used throughout induction, training, appraisal, grievance and disciplinary procedures to highlight and compare the employee's work with what he is expected to do. It also plays a key role in job evaluation, allowing you to compare jobs with each other to set (or upgrade) pay structures within the organization.

The layout and style of a job description vary from one company to another. There are very few universal guidelines that must be followed except that it ought to contain all the relevant facts about the job (so that its full flavour is conveyed to everyone), be no more than two sides long (if it's concise, it is more likely to be read and absorbed), be totally accurate (to avoid subsequent disputes about what's involved), and be easy to understand (you, your colleagues and applicants need to know what it all means).

Draft your job description around these headings:

- The job title
- Responsible to . . .
- Responsible for . . .
- Purpose
- Duties
- Responsibilities
- Signature and date

The job title
Keep this short and simple. Avoid vague, in-house or technical titles. If a job description is used as the basis for job advertisements, as it should be, a potentially confusing or misleading job title may dissuade ideal applicants from applying. It could further encourage totally unsuitable applicants to apply, thus wasting your time and resources.

Responsible to . . .
The job title(s) of the employee's immediate superior(s) needs to be stated here. This too ought to be plain and down to earth. Do not put actual names since they may change jobs in the near future, automatically outdating the job description.

Responsible for . . .
If appropriate, the job titles of the employee's subordinates should be listed under this heading. Again, they must be self-explanatory and names should be avoided.

Purpose
The overall objectives of the job have to be given. Briefly summarize

---

JOB DESCRIPTION

DRIVER OF: SMALL GOODS, BULKY GOODS, ARTICULATED, BAKERY OR MARKET DELIVERY VEHICLE

RESPONSIBLE TO: FOREMAN/TRANSPORT & DEPOT MANAGER

PURPOSE OF JOB:
1. To deliver goods to and from nominated addresses.
2. To drive and use vehicle safely in accordance with current legislation.

DUTIES TO INCLUDE:
1. To load vehicle safely and securely checking items against delivery sheet.
2. To handle goods with care, obtain 'proof of delivery' and return to Depot on completion of deliveries with least possible deviation and/or delay.
3. Return all undelivered goods and delivery sheet to Despatch.

RESPONSIBILITIES:
1. Before leaving Depot carry out driver's daily checks as outlined in your 'Driver's Guide'.
2. Ensure vehicle is not overloaded, if in doubt check on Weighbridge.
3. Check that all documentation, e.g. Clock card, Log sheet, Delivery and call sheets are complete and with driver. Complete same and hand in on return to depot.
4. Record all Vehicle defects in accordance with defects report procedure, and report all accidents in accordance with laid down instructions.
5. To take all possible steps to ensure the safety of vehicle and its load.
6. To present a tidy appearance, wearing uniform provided, and a polite manner at all times.
7. To perform related duties as reasonably allocated.

Signature .... Date ....

Figure 1.1 A job description for a driver

JOB DESCRIPTION

BILLER/CASHIER (SERVICE DESK OR CASH AREA)

RESPONSIBLE TO: SERVICE DESK MANAGER/MERCHANDISE
MANAGER

PURPOSE OF JOB:
1. To receive Sale "Note for Customers" or "Export Plic" from
    assistant together with purchase.
2. To make out bill for type of transaction required, eg. cash
    send, Account or Export, etc. in accordance with the
    Company training instructions.
3. To accept cash and cheques from customers, ring amount
    on cash register, give correct change and cash register
    receipt.
4. To direct customer requiring merchandise, services and
    information in any part of the store.

DUTIES TO INCLUDE:
1. Quick, courteous and businesslike use of telephone.
    Detailed recording of messages or asking Sales Assistant
    (where necessary) to speak to Caller.
2. Maintenance of Service Desk or Cash area-in a elean-and
    tidy manner.
3. Ensuring supplies of documents, packing and wrapping
    materials are readily available.

Figure 1.2   A job description for a biller/cashier

the key role that the employee is expected to play within the
department and company. Ask the employee's immediate superior
and your colleagues for their opinions if necessary.

Duties
All the main duties uncovered during the job analysis should be
outlined as this point. Don't include every conceivable task, though.
A lengthy list can be discouraging for people who are thinking of

Figure 1.2   *continued*

RESPONSIBILITIES:

1. Obtaining cash float, checking amount and putting into cash register ready for store opening at 9.30am.
2. Quick efficient and courteous service to customer for all types of transactions.
3. To ensure that service is given in strict rotation, and so avoid complaints from customers frequently in a hurry.
4. Accurate accounting for all cash, cheques, tokens, copies of bills, or other evidence received in the day's trading in accordance with rules and instructions laid down by the company.
5. Dissection of Sales figures as required by Buyer/Manager of departments within area served by Bill Desk or Cash area.
6. To remain on duty until last customer is served in the area, or transaction is taken over by the Service Desk Manager.
7. Cashing up and paying in to float room at end of day's trading in accordance with company's training instructions.
8. NEVER to leave cash register, or cash and cheques unlocked, or to hand money or goods to anyone without first checking their authority to receive same.
9. To present a well groomed appearance and courteous manner at all times.
10. To perform related duties as reasonably allocated.

Signed .... Date ....

Figure 1.2   *concluded*

applying for the job. Use everyday phrases when describing duties. Colleagues who are unfamiliar with the job may have to explain what it involves, perhaps over the telephone or to an applicant calling in 'on spec'. They – and applicants – might not understand jargon or slang expressions.

JOB DESCRIPTION

STORE DETECTIVE

RESPONSIBLE TO: CHIEF SECURITY OFFICER/DEPUTY CHIEF
                  SECURITY OFFICER

PURPOSE OF JOB:
1. To detect, arrest and initiate criminal proceedings against persons committing arrestable offences against the Company and to obtain written statements from witnesses.
2. To ensure the protection of Company property.

DUTIES TO INCLUDE:
1. To follow up information by observation and/or information.
2. To patrol all floors of the building individually avoiding a regular routine.
3. To give aid to others as required by the circumstances of the incident.
4. To assist and liaise with police and/or other officers in the course of an investigation affecting the Store, staff or customers.
5. To hand safely into custody of police persons detained.

Figure 1.3   A job description for a store detective

Responsibilities

Refer to the employee's main responsibilities at this stage. Once more, stick to the key ones and use suitable language. It is also sensible to add a 'catch-all' phrase at the end such as 'To assist with any other tasks as and when necessary' or 'To perform other duties as reasonably required'. This effectively draws in all those odd duties and responsibilities (too minor and infrequent to list) which you would expect the employee to carry out. Adding this phrase, and perhaps referring to it at an interview, can help to avoid arguments about the employee's role after starting work.

Figure 1.3   *continued*

RESPONSIBILITIES:
1.   To arrest and take offender to Security Office, ensuring that evidence is not disposed of en route. To avoid unnecessary use of force even under provocation.
2.   To relate the evidence to Chief Security Officer or his deputy in the presence of the offender, using an interpreter if necessary.
3.   To accompany the offender together with Police Officer, to Police Station. Prepare Charge on behalf of the Company by signing the 'Charge Sheet'.
4.   To write out statement in accordance with current legislation in duplicate handing top copy to Police.
5.   To give accurate, impartial and lucid evidence in Court.
6.   To take possession of and responsibility for safe custody in Security cupboard of goods and merchandise involved in case.
7.   To investigate and write comprehensive accurate reports and submit for further action.
8.   To ensure that Fire, Security and Company regulations and instructions are adhered to by all persons on the premises.
9.   To present a well groomed business-like appearance especially when giving evidence in Court.
10.   To perform related duties as allocated.

Signature .... Date ....

Figure 1.3   *concluded*

Signature and date

Finally, sign and date the job description. Be prepared to check and update it regularly if it is to be continually useful before *and* after recruitment. Have a look at it whenever you assess the job holder.

Examples of job descriptions for a driver, cashier and store detective are reproduced as Figures 1.1.–1.3, by courtesy of Selfridges Ltd.

Drawing up an employee specification

An employee specification – also known as a job, person or personnel specification – lists the skills, knowledge and experience required to do the job successfully. It can be compiled by studying the duties and responsibilities referred to in the job description and by thinking about the qualities needed to carry out each one properly.

Knowing the type of person you are looking for will help you to decide where to advertise and what to include in job advertisements to attract the right people. On receipt of application forms, letters and curricula vitae, you can compare applicants' stated attributes against your requirements to eliminate those who are obviously unsuitable. Interviews and tests can be based around the employee specification as well. During these selection methods, you may use it as an assessment form, making notes about or grading each candidate alongside the various qualities wanted. After you have taken on a new employee, it is especially useful for staff appraisal, enabling you to judge how he is progressing and whether you have chosen the most suitable person for the job.

There are several important guidelines to consider when drawing up an employee specification. Try not to over-idealize and set so many requirements that you are unable to find such a perfect person (thus incurring more time and effort if you have to start the recruitment process again). Be both realistic and relevant: divide your requirements into 'essentials' (those that are absolutely vital if the job is to be done well) and 'desirables' (those that you'd prefer the successful candidate to have but won't insist upon). You could also include 'contra-indications' whereby applicants are automatically disqualified if they have these particular characteristics (even though all the 'essentials' and 'desirables' may have been met).

Make sure the qualities you seek are easy to measure and assess from reading application forms, letters and curricula vitae (handwriting, spelling, writing ability, and so on), interviewing candidates (appearance, speech, ability to converse, and so forth) and taking up references (previous work record, experience, and so on). Some qualities (intelligence, personality) can be hard to evaluate and are often best assessed through selection tests which may not be readily available or cost-effective, especially for smaller businesses.

Use precise language when writing out requirements. Steer clear of words such as 'average' or 'good' which can be interpreted differently by job seekers reading your advertisements and even your

Be specific

colleagues who may be responsible for pre-screening applicants on your behalf. Be specific – replace vague phrases ('must be well educated') with definite ones ('must be educated to degree level or its equivalent').

Do not discriminate unlawfully when drafting an employee specification. The Sex Discrimination Act (1975) and the Race Relations Act (1976) make it illegal to discriminate on the grounds of sex, marital status or race in the field of employment. To do so could lead to an industrial tribunal, financial compensation being paid and much unwelcome publicity for your firm (perhaps unsettling your existing workforce and dissuading job hunters from applying for your job vacancies in the future).

'Direct discrimination' exists where a person (or persons) is treated less favourably because of their sex, marital status or race than another (of a different sex, marital status or race) is or would be treated in the same or similar circumstances, for example, an employer who only ever recruits men to fill management vacancies and single people for jobs that involve overnight stays away from home.

'Indirect discrimination' – of prime significance here – is where requirements are set which, although they may appear fair, are unlawful because a smaller proportion of people of a particular sex, marital status or race are likely to be able to meet them. Such requirements are only lawful if they can be shown to be justifiable. For example, demanding a high standard of spoken English may lead to a smaller number of members of certain racial groups applying for the job. An employer would need to be sure (and might even have to prove it to an industrial tribunal if a complaint were made) that this requirement was necessary to do the job well and not included simply to reduce the number of applications from these racial groups.

Sometimes sex or race may be a 'genuine occupational qualification' and can therefore be included lawfully in an employee specification. A model or an actor may have to be of a particular sex or race for authenticity. A man or a woman might need to be employed to preserve decency or privacy, perhaps in the case of a changing room attendant at a swimming pool. A job in a single-sex prison or hospital could legitimately be made available only to a person of that sex.

Try to avoid discriminating unfairly in any way. A minimum or maximum age limit should be established only if it is essential, perhaps to comply with the law ('must be over 18 to sell wines and spirits'). Physical disability ought to be an issue only if it means that person cannot perform the job properly, rather than because you find his handicap embarrassing or inconvenient. Even if his disability is a problem, it can often be overcome (and should be if he is the best person for the job). Perhaps various tasks can be re-allocated or adjustments made to premises or equipment. By law, if you employ 20 or more people, at least 3 per cent of them should be registered disabled people. Bear this in mind when recruiting. Gay applicants ought to be treated fairly at all times too. Judge every person on their ability to do the job, not according to your personal likes and dislikes.

Avoiding discrimination is a theme which runs throughout this book, being referred to whenever relevant. The key points are drawn together in Appendix A where the Sex Discrimination Act, the Race Relations Act and The Disabled Persons (Employment) Acts are summarized. The Equal Opportunities Commission, the Commission for Racial Equality and the Department of Employment Group – all committed to working towards the elimination of discrimination and to promote equality of opportunity – also publish codes of practice which are reproduced in Appendix B. You may find it helpful to look at these now, before writing out your employee specification.

Gather your 'essential' and 'desirable' requirements (and any contra-indications) together under a set of headings. The most popular framework for this is the Seven-Point Plan devised by the late Professor Alec Rodger of the National Institute of Industrial Psychology, as follows:

- Physical make-up
- Attainments
- Intelligence
- Special aptitudes
- Interests
- Disposition
- Circumstances

Physical make-up

First, think about the physical characteristics that the successful employee 'must' or 'should' have. Which of these are important?

- Appearance
- Speech
- Health
- Eyesight
- Hearing

- Age
- Sex
- Race
- Build

Appearance and speech will probably be far more significant if the employee deals with customers than if he works behind the scenes where they may be relatively unimportant. A satisfactory bill of health (according to the rigours of the particular job) is always relevant though. You don't want to employ someone who is continually off sick. Ask a previous employer about a candidate's health, attendance record and so on when taking up references. Arrange a medical if the job is especially demanding. If appropriate, eyesight and hearing may have to be tested professionally too. Only set an age requirement if absolutely necessary. Be careful to avoid discriminating on the grounds of sex, race or disability. Be aware that a height or weight requirement may favour one sex more than the other. Men tend to be taller and heavier than women. Only include the requirement if it is justifiable.

Attainments
Move on to detail those attainments needed to do the job well. Consider these areas:

- Education
- Training
- Qualifications
- Work experience.

If you feel qualifications are relevant, try to set them at an appropriate level. Taking on an underqualified person may mean he is unable to cope with the pressures of the job. Employing an overqualified person can be a serious mistake as well. He could become bored and restless in a job that rarely stretches him. When asking for qualifications add the phrase 'or their equivalent'. Applicants who have lived abroad may have different – but equally good – qualifications. Should you believe previous work experience is necessary, be willing to accept a variety of backgrounds that could have led to the acquisition of key skills and knowledge. Previous employment in the same (or a similar) type of job or company should never automatically be listed as 'essential'.

Intelligence

Next, think about the employee's intelligence. Perhaps you'll be looking for:

- logical thought
- reasoning ability
- a good memory
- wide general knowledge.

Think carefully before setting requirements under this heading. Intelligence can be difficult – if not impossible – to measure and compare with any accuracy simply by reading application forms and interviewing candidates, especially if you are untrained and inexperienced. You will need to set up costly and time-consuming intelligence tests run by test consultants or yourself (only after extensive training into the appropriate methods and techniques) if you wish to gauge such qualities properly. You may not feel this is worthwhile, particularly for lower-grade jobs. (Read General aptitude tests on page 113 before making such requirements. You'll then know all that's involved in assessing them.)

Special aptitudes

Decide whether there are any specific skills that are needed to handle the job, such as:

- verbal aptitude
- mechanical ability
- manual dexterity
- numerical aptitude
- writing ability.

If strictly relevant, you should arrange tests to establish and compare the respective abilities of different candidates (see Specific aptitude tests, page 118).

Interests

It may be prudent to seek an employee who has leisure pursuits that relate to the job in some way:

- literary

- social
- artistic
- sporting.

Such interests are easy to check by reading application forms, letters and curricula vitae and by questioning candidates during interviews.

Disposition

Often, the successful employee will need a particular temperament. Most employers would want to recruit staff with some (or all) of the following attributes:

- common sense
- team spirit
- calm manner
- methodical nature
- mature attitude
- sense of humour
- tact
- discretion.

These qualities can be hard to measure especially in an interview where the candidate will be on his best behaviour. Once more, tests may need to be conducted if you set requirements in this area (see Personality tests, page 138).

Circumstances

Finally, consider the employee's general circumstances. Possibly, he ought to have some or all of these:

- his own transport
- a clean driving licence
- local residence
- his own telephone.

Any other essential or desirable requirements or contra-indications should also be detailed here. As with all requirements, remember to keep them relevant, easy to measure, precisely worded and non-discriminatory.

Examples of employee specifications for a driver, cashier and store detective are given in Figures 1.4–1.6. Before looking at them, turn

Sex (where essential) *Age/Range*

EMPLOYEE SPECIFICATION

JOB TITLE: DRIVER OF ARTICULATED DELIVERY VEHICLE

ESSENTIAL REQUIREMENTS:
- Must present a tidy appearance, being willing to wear the uniform provided during working hours.
- Must possess a clean HGV licence.
- Must have a polite manner to deal with customers.
- Must be able to work evenings and weekends as required.

DESIRABLE REQUIREMENTS:
- Should have GCSE 'C' grade passes (or the equivalent) in Mathematics and English Language.
- Should have previous experience of delivering and collecting goods and handling customers and documentation.

CONTRA-INDICATION:
- Must be no evidence of recurring ill health over the past 5 years which may affect the ability to drive an articulated vehicle in a safe manner.

Signature .... Date ....

Figure 1.4   An employee specification for a driver

back to Figures 1.1–1.3 to see the job descriptions that they are based on. Think about the requirements you would set and compare them with those listed.

Evaluating future needs

Of course, recruitment must not be carried out just to satisfy your immediate staff needs. You should be seeking someone who will stay with the company on a long-term basis, adjusting to the different demands of the job as it inevitably develops over the years. Also, he

---

EMPLOYEE SPECIFICATION

JOB TITLE: SERVICE DESK CASHIER

ESSENTIAL REQUIREMENTS:
- Must present a well groomed appearance and be willing to wear the company uniform at work.
- Must have a polite and courteous manner for dealing with the general public.
- Must be able to work overtime, especially during the Summer and New Year sales.

DESIRABLE REQUIREMENTS:
- Should have 5 GCSE "C" grade passes or the equivalent preferably in English Language and Mathematics.
- Should have previous experience of shop work, using a till and handling cash.
- Should be interested in meeting and helping people.
- Should show some evidence of a calm and tactful manner.

CONTRA-INDICATIONS:
- None in particular.

Signature .... Date ....

Figure 1.5 An employee specification for a cashier

should be able enough to be transferred or promoted to other posts as and when they become available. In short, the recruitment of any employee must form part of a general employment strategy.

A manpower plan involves studying the make-up of the present workforce, assessing the forthcoming changes and influences which will affect it and then calculating and working towards the future workforce that is required. Such a plan has many benefits. It allows you to devise a long-term recruitment programme, selecting staff to meet both present and future needs. Career moves can be anticipated well in advance, with you pencilling in who will move where and when. Training for those employees scheduled for transfer or promotion

---

```
EMPLOYEE SPECIFICATION

JOB TITLE:  STORE DETECTIVE

ESSENTIAL REQUIREMENTS:
  ● Must present a business-like appearance.
  ● Must show some evidence of common sense and a calm
    manner under provocation, perhaps through appropriate
    work experience.
  ● Must be willing to "floor-walk" throughout working hours
    as required.
  ● Must be willing to give evidence in court.

DESIRABLE REQUIREMENTS:
  ● Should have previous work experience of the same or
    similar nature.
  ● Should have some knowledge of criminal law through
    qualifications, training or previous employment.

CONTRA-INDICATIONS:
  ● Must not have a criminal record.
  ● Must not have any health problems which may affect
    constant mobility or the ability to spot and apprehend shop
    lifters.

Signature ................................................................ Date .........................
```

Figure 1.6   An employee specification for a store detective

may be carried out over an appropriate period of time, rather than
'on the job' as so often happens. If overmanning looks likely, distressing redundancies can be avoided through natural wastage, early
retirement and so on.

Drawing up an accurate and useful manpower plan is difficult. It
is notoriously hard to see into the future, with some factors such as
political and economic changes impossible to predict with certainty.
Nevertheless, even a tentative and slightly speculative plan is far
better than no plan at all. Recruiting staff on a day-to-day basis is a

recipe for disaster. At some stage the company may wish to expand into new products or markets. It is unlikely to be able to do this successfully if it hasn't carefully manoeuvred the right employees into the right places, ready to implement its policies.

Begin drafting an appropriate plan by evaluating your existing workforce. Consider them in terms of the total numbers employed by the company and in each department (sales, production, accounts and so on). Then look at the types and levels of different jobs, appraising employees with regard to age, skills, knowledge and experience. You should be able to make full use of job descriptions and employee specifications here.

Following this, you need to consider the natural changes that will occur within the workforce over the duration of the plan, which will usually be for up to five years as assessment beyond this entails too much guesswork. Estimate the number of likely resignations (check your labour turnover records), retirements (bear in mind the ages of your present employees), transfers and promotions (based upon resignations and retirements).

There will also be many influences, both internal and external, which will affect the types and numbers of employees needed over the coming months and years. You should always be aware of the company's intentions for the future. Such developments as expansion, diversification, changes in the organizational structure and the introduction of new technology take time to come to fruition. Progress should be carefully monitored with the effects on the work force being considered at every stage.

External factors have to be thought about as well. The trade or industry in which you operate may be static or, more likely, could be contracting or expanding. The economic situation – in particular, inflation and interest rates – might alter in the near future. The political climate may change with new approaches being adopted towards various issues. Society could have different expectations of your company, perhaps wanting you to go 'green'. Not only will all these have a direct influence on your business policies and procedures; they'll affect your employees too.

Also take into account the availability of labour locally and/or nationally, as appropriate. In most industrialized countries the number of school, college and university leavers entering the job market is falling rapidly. It is becoming increasingly difficult to recruit top quality youngsters and this will have an inevitable knock-on effect throughout your company over the years. Fortunately, in many countries this drop is largely equalled by an expanding number of working mothers and early retired people looking for employment. The composition of your workforce will thus, almost certainly, slowly alter.

On the basis of these changes and influences, you can calculate the workforce needed in two, three or five years (in terms of total numbers, ages, skills and so on). Look again at your present employees whom you believe will still be with you, deciding which can be moved across and upwards as necessary. They may then be trained and developed accordingly. Prospective employees will need to be recruited at appropriate times with you referring to the manpower plan beforehand so you know the qualities desired now *and* in the future, as well as how and when they are expected to progress.

Monitor your manpower plan constantly, checking and amending it in the light of new developments and/or anticipated changes. A thorough quarterly or six-monthly review, according to individual circumstances, may be a good idea.

Summary

Question   How should the recruitment process begin?
Answer   It must start with a comprehensive evaluation of the job so that you can decide on its future and the type of person required to do it. A job analysis ought to be carried out, after which a job description and an employee specification should be drafted.

Question   What does a job analysis involve?
Answer   It entails collecting as much information as possible about a job – its function, position in the organization, main duties, work environment and the qualities needed to do it well.

Question   What is a job description?
Answer   It is a document outlining the purpose, duties and responsibilities of a job. Based on job analysis notes, it plays an invaluable role throughout recruitment.

Question   What is an employee specification?
Answer   It is a document listing the skills, knowledge and experience necessary for the job. Drawn up after studying job analysis notes and the job description, there is little hope of finding the right person without it.

Question How can future staff needs be estimated?

Answer A manpower plan has to be prepared. By looking at the existing workforce and thinking about the possible changes and influences on it, you should be able to assess the likely future workforce required. Staff can then be recruited on the basis of this forecast.

2 Seeking applicants

Having analysed the job and drawn up a detailed job description and employee specification, you must decide where to look for potential applicants who would be able to do the job well. If future staff requirements have been planned for some time, you may know of existing employees who could be transferred or promoted. Alternatively, you might go outside the company to fill the vacancy. Both courses of action – and their respective benefits and drawbacks – need to be considered carefully. You then ought to know how to assess and select the most appropriate sources of recruitment which will reach the people you want to apply for the job.

Recruiting internally or externally

Recruiting from among your current workforce offers many advantages. Seeing your employees at work on a day-to-day basis will enable you to evaluate their particular strengths and weaknesses accurately and choose the most suitable person for the position. The selected employee, with experience of company policies and practices, should find it relatively easy to adjust and quickly settle into his new role. Minimal time, effort and money will need to be spent on induction and training.

Knowing that the company recruits from within ought to please and motivate all your staff. They will feel important and highly valued since it appears that you immediately turn to them whenever a vacancy occurs. Their work rate and performance should improve as well as they will realize that increasing job opportunities are available to them if they are industrious and successful at their jobs.

There can be disadvantages with internal recruitment, however. Too often, an employee is transferred or promoted simply because he is next in line for the post. Although he could have many admirable qualities, this does not necessarily mean he is the right choice for this position. His specific skills, knowledge and experience, however extensive they may be, might not match those listed so precisely on your employee specification. Unsuited to the job and unable to meet its demands, his work and morale (and those of the employees around him) will suffer. Lateness, unauthorized absences and conflict between him and his fellow workers could occur.

Even if an employee is perfect for the job – perhaps he was originally taken on with a view to filling the post in due course – he should still have to apply and progress through a complete (and genuine) recruitment process along with other internal applicants. Automatic promotion, without reference to or consideration of other interested employees, might create anger and frustration among those who believe they could handle the job and would have liked to have applied for it.

Constantly recruiting from inside the company can sometimes result in a severe shortage of new ideas and developments. If top posts are always taken by long-serving employees steeped in company traditions and methods, then it is probable that the same attitudes and approaches will forever be adopted towards business matters. In an ever-changing business environment, such a policy could be detrimental, if not fatal.

You should recognize the primary benefit of recruiting from outside the company's present workforce. Different backgrounds, fresh thoughts and new opinions can combine with existing experience and knowledge to produce more effective solutions to business issues. Also, of course, there may not be a member of staff capable of doing the job properly. The necessary qualities required just might not exist in any of your employees.

Think about the drawbacks of external recruitment, however. It is invariably a lengthy process, taking far longer than when only internal applicants are being considered. Studying external sources of recruitment, drafting eye-catching, well-phrased advertisements, reading and replying to applications and arranging and conducting interviews and tests cannot be rushed if the right person is to be selected.

In addition, it can prove to be extremely costly to recruit an outsider. Many sources of recruitment are expensive to use. Employing experts to run selection tests also involves considerable financial outlay. The time invested in external recruitment, which could have been spent on other matters, should not be overlooked either.

It is far more difficult to choose a suitable person from external applicants about whom you know little or nothing than from internal applicants whom you know well. Often, you are making a decision merely on the basis of an application form and an interview. A person who writes well or performs well at a face-to-face meeting may not necessarily be able to do the job competently. If you make a mistake, the effects can be traumatic (conflict, ill feeling, resignation or dismissal and so on).

Internal recruitment is generally considered to be better, assuming you're aware of and can overcome the disadvantages, as it tends to be quicker, cheaper and more reliable. External recruitment may be used if no-one is available internally or new blood needs to be injected into the company.

Assessing sources of recruitment

Whether recruiting internally or externally, you must study carefully the wide variety of individual sources of recruitment that are available to you (see Internal sources and External sources, pages 29 and 31 respectively). When looking at each, ask yourself the following questions. Consider using that particular source of recruitment only if you can answer 'yes' to all three of them.

- Will it reach the right people?
- Will it reach the right numbers?
- Will it be at the right price?

Will it reach the right people?

The main criterion by which you ought to judge each source must be whether it will put you in touch with potentially suitable applicants. No matter how competent you are at drawing up application forms, screening applications, conducting interviews and running tests, it is all largely irrelevant if you do not have a good field of applicants to choose from. Your subsequent recruitment process, thorough though it may be, will only confirm that you have a group of unsatisfactory applicants, none of whom can be transformed into an ideal employee however hard you might try.

To decide if a source is appropriate in the circumstances, read through the job description and employee specification. Think about where that level and type of job vacancy is usually publicized. Check the other vacancies promoted through that source. If in doubt, talk to employees in the same or similar positions to discover which sources of recruitment they used when they were job hunting.

Will it reach the right numbers?

It is not enough just to get potentially ideal applicants to apply for the post. They must also do so in the right numbers. Too few, and you'll find that by the time you've arranged interviews, one will already have obtained a job, another won't turn up, two will be unsuitable and the only remaining candidate will turn down your job offer. Thus, you'll have to begin the whole process again. Too many and you'll incur the extra time and expense involved with reading and responding to all the applications. Faced with a large pile of correspondence, you may also be tempted not to study them all properly and could therefore overlook several would-be employees.

Although opinion varies considerably as to the number of applicants required, you'll probably want to invite around half a dozen for an interview and tests. Additional applicants will therefore simply increase your recruitment costs. Unfortunately, you won't know the number of suitable and – of equal importance – unsuitable applicants who will contact you until after you've used the source. Save time and expenditure by talking to others who have been involved with that source of recruitment. Ask for their advice and heed it. If possible, check company records too just in case the source was used by another department in the past. Evaluate the results. (Be aware that the way in which advertisements are designed and phrased will affect the type and number of applicants – see Chapter 3).

Will it be at the right price?

Always take into account the cost, in terms of both time and money, of a specific source of recruitment. It should be in proportion to the job concerned and its value to the company. Balance the expense against the type and number of people that it will reach. Obtain information from all sources available to you prior to proceeding.

Chat to others who have used the source before to see if they feel it was value for money. If necessary, discuss your ideas with colleagues before making a final choice.

Internal sources

Of the various internal sources of recruitment used, these are the most common:

- personal recommendations
- noticeboards
- newsletters
- memoranda

Personal recommendations

You or your colleagues will probably know of several employees who could successfully fill the vacancy. Approaching them may be a highly efficient method of recruitment but will almost certainly offend other workers who would have wished to have been considered for the job. To keep everyone happy, make sure that potentially suitable employees are informed of the vacancy so that they can apply. Make certain that anyone else who is likely to be interested is told about it as well. Never simply go straight to the person you've earmarked for the job if you wish to maintain a contented team. Also, keep an open mind about all applicants throughout the recruitment process. Don't just go through the motions with those you didn't originally think of. They may prove to be most suitable for the vacant position.

Noticeboards

This can be a convenient and simple method of passing on important messages to your staff. A job advertisement pinned to a noticeboard will probably be seen and read by a sufficient number of appropriate employees at little or no cost. However, many of your staff will probably not learn of the vacancy in this way either because the noticeboard is poorly located or is so full of outdated notices that they don't bother to look at it, as they assume there is nothing new to find out.

If you're thinking of using a noticeboard, and it can be a good method if approached properly, ensure that it is well sited. Consider placing it inside a restroom, by the vending machine where staff queue for drinks and snacks or in the canteen where they stand in line waiting to be served. Wherever you put it, be certain that it can be seen by everyone. Bear in mind that you might be accused of unlawful discrimination if a notice were located near male or female toilets where only one sex (or predominantly more of one sex) would be likely to come across it.

Having placed the noticeboard where all your staff have an equal opportunity to see it, you must then get them to study it. They will only do this if they know that just important, topical notices are on display. Put a junior employee in charge of the noticeboard, asking him to keep it uncluttered and up to date. Also, attention must be paid to the design and contents of the notice if it is to catch the eye and make the employee read on and then want to apply for the job. (see Chapter 3).

Newsletters

Many companies regularly produce in-house newsletters, magazines or journals for their staff to read. You could take space within the forthcoming issue to promote the vacancy and encourage interested employees to apply. It is hoped that the latest company newsheet is read avidly by all staff thus ensuring that every one of them is aware of the job. Unfortunately, this is not always so because it is sometimes not circulated widely enough and employees may find it boring and choose not to read it. Furthermore, if publication is only occasional, or even irregular, then there is little point in advertising a vacancy you wish to fill as soon as possible.

Only use your company newsletter as a source of recruitment if you are convinced that everybody will see a copy. Department heads could all be given a batch to be handed out to each individual team member. Be sure that the newsletter is interesting enough to be read, by dividing it into subject sections with up-to-date information interspersed with staff comments, competitions, humour, cartoons and a swap shop page. This may make it lively and popular. Consider the timing of the next issue too (can you afford to leave the job vacant until publication?) Give some thought to how the advertisement will attract attention as well (see Chapter 3).

Memoranda

Possibly the best way of circulating news of a job vacancy is to send memoranda to department managers to read out to their teams or to write to all employees, perhaps enclosing memoranda in wage packets, if appropriate. This should guarantee that anyone remotely interested in applying for the position knows enough about it to do so. Bear in mind, however, that it can be a time-consuming process to contact staff individually, especially if you have a large workforce. You also need to think about the way in which the memorandum is phrased so that the job appeals to likely applicants (see Chapter 3).

External sources

There are many different sources of recruitment to choose from if you are seeking to recruit from outside the company, for example:

- word of mouth
- notices
- job centres
- private agencies and consultants
- educational institutions
- careers centres
- the press
- radio
- television

Word of mouth

Your existing employees may have friends and relatives who would like to apply for the job. Recruiting in this way appears to be simple, inexpensive and convenient. By chatting to intermediary members of staff, both you and would-be applicants can obtain more background information about each other than is normal. This might help you to reach a selection decision more quickly and ensures that the new recruit doesn't begin work under any illusions about what is involved, which is so often the cause of subsequent unrest.

However, both the Equal Opportunities Commission and the Commission for Racial Equality state that you should never use word of mouth as a sole or initial source of recruitment if your workforce is wholly or predominantly of one sex or racial group. In such circumstances, it is considered likely that this will exclude or disproportionately reduce the number of people of the alternative sex or other racial groups applying for the job. Accordingly, you may be accused of unlawful discrimination.

Also, employing friends and relatives of present employees may

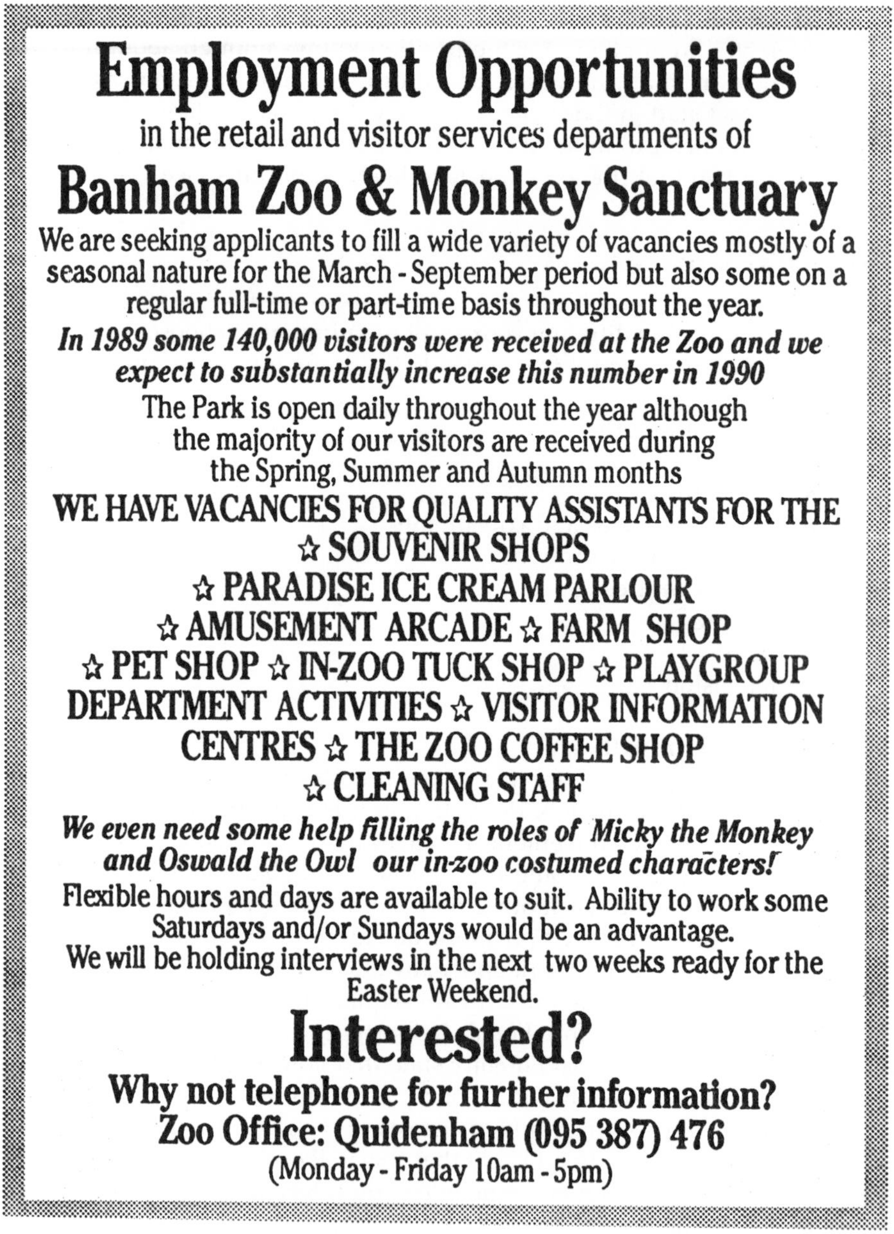

Figure 2.1 A recruitment poster for a zoo

Bettys **TAYLORS**

CAREERS FAIR

THURSDAY 30th AUGUST 1990

We have over 700 people at our Tea & Coffee Factory, Bakery, Bettys Café Tea Rooms, Bettys By Post and Head Office. On Thursday 30th August 7.00pm - 9.00pm we will be holding a Careers Fair in the Spindler Room at Bettys Harrogate.

Staff and Managers from all areas of our business will be available to discuss a wide range of careers with you in:

Catering . Retail . Trainee Management
Baking . Confectionery . Manufacturing

We also have both Full and Part Time vacancies for the following positions:

Assistant Managers . Sales Assistants . Cashiers
Cooks . Chefs . Kitchen Assistants
Waiters . Waitresses . Cleaners

As a trainee you will have the opportunity to be sponsored for external training courses, furthering your education.

If you would like to find out more about careers within the company, or are interested in any of the job vacancies listed above please call in for an informal chat on Thursday 30th August anytime between 7.00pm - 9.00pm.

EVERYONE WELCOME

Figure 2.2 A recruitment poster for a factory

be imprudent because you cannot be certain that they are as competent as your staff say they are. Many people are blind to the faults of their close friends or loved relatives. Cliques may develop, too, with a harmful effect on general team morale.

Notices

Displaying notices in and around business premises is a simple and often overlooked method of advertising a job vacancy. They should be seen by a large number of passers-by, some actively looking for work. It can also be inexpensive, with a 'notice' varying from a carefully handwritten postcard up to a professionally produced poster. Pay attention to the appearance and contents of the notice if you want the right people to apply (see Chapter 3). Two notices that met with considerable success when displayed outside business premises are reproduced as Figures 2.1 and 2.2, courtesy of Banham Zoo Ltd in Norfolk and Betty's Café Tea Rooms Ltd in Yorkshire.

Job centres

Most large towns have a job centre which offers employers a free recruitment service, trying to match their vacancies to job seekers. Staff will note information about a post and the type of person sought and then advertise the vacancy on noticeboards within their premises. Details can also be passed on to other job centres, perhaps across the region or in another area of the country, if there are skills shortages in the immediate locality.

Job centre employees can further help if requested to do so by issuing and assessing application forms and thus weeding out those applicants who are obviously unsuitable for the position. Shortlisted candidates are then sent on for the employer to interview on his business premises, although a quiet room can be made available at the job centre if necessary.

Should you be planning to use a job centre – and they are successful at reaching large numbers of job hunters at all levels at no charge – then pay a visit in person to discuss your requirements. Job centres are often accused of sending hopelessly unsuitable candidates to an employer, thus wasting his time and resources. This can happen because staff have been given insufficient information about the job and person required by the employer.

Avoid this problem by discussing the job in detail with staff at the job centre and supplying company literature and a job description for them to read and hand out to genuinely interested applicants. Talk about the type of person you want to employ, running through the essential and desirable criteria and giving them an employee specification so that they can screen properly. Draft advertisements and application forms for them to use. Make sure that they know exactly what they are expected to do at all times: hand out application forms along with company literature and a job description, compare completed forms with the employee specification, telephone you whenever an applicant appears potentially suitable and so on. If you fail to do this, you only have yourself to blame if the recruitment process goes awry.

Private agencies and consultants

There are various types of private organization that can help you to find the right person for a particular job. *Employment agencies* exist in many towns and cities. Some handle all general vacancies from junior up to supervisory level while others specialize in various occupations such as accountancy, clerical or computer personnel. Since they maintain a register of job seekers, they initially attempt to find applicants from this list. They might further promote the vacancy on their premises, in newspapers or on the radio or television through the Oracle Teletext Service. A shortlist will be drawn up by reading through applications and conducting interviews on your behalf. Although fees vary, you should expect to pay around 10 to 15 per cent of the annual salary offered if a suitable person is found for you. This will be partly refundable if he leaves within a certain period of time. For temporary staff, you would normally be charged an hourly, daily or weekly rate by the agency. They will then pay the employee.

Recruitment agencies are similar to employment agencies in the services that they offer. The main difference is that recruitment agencies tend to operate at a higher level, concentrating on technical, managerial and executive appointments. Accordingly, increased time, effort and expertise is needed to compile a quality shortlist. This will be reflected in the fees charged, often between 18 and 22 per cent of the annual salary. Again, a proportion of this may be refundable if the employee proves to be unsatisfactory and subsequently departs.

Search consultants, also known as 'headhunters', specialize in finding candidates for senior positions. They normally headhunt people currently at work in similar posts, possibly at rival companies. Discreet approaches, perhaps by telephone, are made direct to the persons involved. Such a process is time-consuming and requires considerable tact and diplomacy if it is to be successful. Charges may be in excess of 30 per cent of the annual salary.

If you are thinking of employing a private agency or consultant, talk to business associates to see which ones they have used and can personally vouch for. A recommendation is often the safest way of making a good choice. Alternatively, approach the appropriate professional body, as listed in Appendix C, which will provide a list of reputable members in your region.

Shortlist three of four agencies that seem likely to be able to handle the assignment well. Contact them to discover whether they have sufficient experience of dealing with this type of vacancy. They might specialize in another area or at a different level. Find out which other companies they have worked for and ask for permission to approach them for references. Always get in touch with their referees and listen and assess their comments carefully.

Meet the person who will be doing the work should you decide to commission the agency. Too often, an initial meeting takes place with a partner who, after obtaining the assignment, passes you on to a junior in whom you have little confidence. See him beforehand and be certain that you have sufficient faith in him to be able to establish a close working relationship.

Find out how the agency would set about this particular assignment. Be wary of those who brashly promise to give you a lengthy list of candidates very quickly. It may sound impressive but suggests that they are simply pulling names from a register (perhaps of dubious quality) and are not actively searching for and screening applicants properly. A good shortlist will take time to compile.

Establish the cost of commissioning the agency – is it in proportion with the importance of the job to your company? Never be afraid to negotiate over the fee as it ought to be open to discussion. Insist on a good refund system in case the new recruit resigns or needs to be dismissed shortly after joining. Usually, you'd be looking for a full refund if he leaves within the first month, 50 per cent in the following month and so on. Also, ask for a free replacement warranty for up to six months. Often, it can take that long before you really know whether a new recruit is truly suitable or not.

When employing an agency or consultant, make sure that they know exactly what they are expected to do: draw up advertisements and application forms for you, place advertisements, issue application forms and so forth; and how they should do it: base advertisements and application forms on the job description and employee specification, screen by referring to the employee specification and so on. Give them full, up-to-date information about the job and person required. Supply all details and instructions in writing to avoid subsequent misunderstandings and disagreements.

Keep in touch throughout the recruitment process to ensure that the agency is following instructions and doing its job well. Also ensure that they are maintaining equality of opportunity and avoiding unlawful discrimination against applicants of a particular sex, marital status or racial group. All applicants should be judged solely on their ability to do the job.

Educational institutions

Those companies which require a steady intake of young persons for new Youth Training to trainee management positions ought to establish and maintain close contact with schools, colleges and universities. This is now especially important bearing in mind the much publicized drop in the number of youngsters entering the job market in the early to mid-1990s.

The advantages of setting up close links are that you know exactly who your audience is (which cannot be truly guaranteed with other sources of recruitment) and should further be assured of a steady flow of reasonably suitable applicants for relatively little financial outlay. Of course, the number and quality of applicants may vary from one educational establishment to another often according to how the individual establishments and their staff view their role in the job-seeking process. Some are vigorously active in helping their students to find work; others are largely indifferent.

You can do much yourself to ensure a good supply of young applicants. Get in touch with the school, college or university to discover the names of the staff who should be contacted. These may include heads of departments, individual teachers or lecturers, careers counsellors or librarians. Pay them a visit to talk about your company, the variety of job vacancies available and the type of youngsters you're looking for. Keep them well supplied throughout the academic year (September to June) with promotional literature in the form of posters, brochures, catalogues, press releases and so on, so that your company remains prominent in their and their students' minds all the time. Give them full details of job vacancies, job advertisements, job description, employee specification, application forms and so on as they arise.

Also, you might advertise your company and its products or

services within student guidebooks and magazines. At schools, you could offer to talk to imminent leavers about your company and industry. You may even become a part-time lecturer at your local college of higher and further education. Consider offering students work placements throughout the year to help them gain work experience. All these approaches will give your company a high profile, ensuring, hopefully, that students automatically turn to you when they begin job hunting.

Careers centres

Many employers overlook their local council's careers advisory service as a useful source of recruitment because they believe it only exists to give school and college leavers advice about the careers they want to pursue. Of course, this is one of its primary aims but it also tries to match job-seeking youngsters with job vacancies in the area. Thus your local careers centre acts as an intermediary between companies and school and college leavers looking for work. As such, it must be worth contacting if you have a job which could be done by a young person.

Similar in many respects to a job centre, it offers a free service to employers. Key information is noted and staff advertise the vacancy in their reception area and contact those youngsters whom they know who appear to match your employee specification. All applicants can be pre-screened by trained staff with only the most suitable being sent to you for a final selection interview.

To avoid having totally inappropriate candidates being forwarded to you, remember to discuss fully your needs with careers centre employees. Give them details of your company as well as a job description, employee specification and application forms, if appropriate. They can only be as good as you let them be.

The press

Advertising for new staff through the press has proved successful for many companies. With such a wide range of titles available, it is relatively easy to pick one or more which reaches the correct type and number of people. Choose between *local newspapers*, *national newspapers* and *trade magazines*. All will put you in touch with a different audience.

Local newspapers, read by a large cross-section of the immediate population, may be most suitable if you believe there is sufficient talent in the area. National newspapers, with their mass circulations and differing attitudes to news coverage appealing to various tastes, could be better should you feel you need to look further afield, perhaps to fill a senior position. Trade magazines, often underestimated as a useful source of recruitment, might be worth considering if you have to recruit someone for a specialized job, which possibly requires previous experience of your particular industry.

Newspapers, whether local or national, offer several benefits to recruitment advertisers. Most have special job vacancy sections which job-seeking readers will automatically turn to. Local, daily or evening newspapers typically run an extra jobs supplement one day or evening every week where the majority of current vacancies will be detailed. National newspapers often carry separate groups of employment opportunities – secretarial, educational, overseas and so on – for each day of the week. Therefore experienced job hunters know when and where to find vacancies of interest to them.

Additional benefits include prompt publication (normally, an advertisement can be accepted today for publication tomorrow or the day after), the inclusion of slightly amended advertisements in different editions (useful for measuring responses to alternative designs and contents, see Monitoring results, page 70) and – of some significance – assistance in the creation of advertisements (see Chapter 3).

Naturally, there are some drawbacks to newspaper advertising. It is expensive in relation to other, often equally good sources such as job and careers centres, which advertise free. Line advertisements, where text runs on line after line under a classified heading such as 'Situations Vacant', cost perhaps £1.50 to £2.50 per column line in a local newspaper and £15 to £25 in a national newspaper. These are approximate 1991 figures, exclusive of VAT, and will vary considerably from one newspaper to another according to circulation. A one column, 10-line advert might therefore cost around £15 to £25 (plus VAT) locally, £150 to £200 (plus VAT) nationally.

Display advertisements are set within their own borders, with a heading and different print from other advertisements around them. Known as semi-display advertisements when placed beneath a classified title such as 'Recruitment' they cost from £4 to £12 per single column centimetre in a local newspaper, £75 to £100 per 'scc' in a national newspaper (again, these are general 1991 rates, exclusive of VAT, and will differ from one newspaper to another). A three-column wide, 10-centimetre deep advertisement could thus cost about £120 to £360 (plus VAT) locally, £2250 to £3000 (plus VAT) nationally.

Other drawbacks of newspaper advertising include a high level of wastage (the vast majority of readers will not be job hunting) and a short life span (the daily or evening newspaper is invariably discarded at the end of the day). A short series of advertisements, incurring extra expense, may sometimes be required, and multiplying one advert by three or four starts to make this source prohibitively costly.

Trade magazines could be a better way of recruiting staff, depending upon your circumstances. Most will include employment advertisements within a classified section which will be read by a small but select and interested number of people. Advertisement rates tend to be similar to those of local newspapers (perhaps £5 to £10 plus VAT per single column centimetre), help can be given in designing advertisements and – worth thinking about – the magazine will be around far longer than a daily newspaper, for perhaps one to three months.

There are some disadvantages, however. The financial outlay is still considerable. More cost-effective options may be open to you. Also, if the magazine is published bi-monthly or even quarterly, you may have to wait some time before your advertisement is seen. You might wish to fill the vacancy as soon as possible.

Should you believe press advertising is right for you, talk to fellow business owners and managers who have adopted this approach to find out their views and which particular newspapers and magazines they had the most success with. Never simply advertise in your favourite newspaper unless you're certain it will be read by the people you want to apply for the job.

Obtain the address, telephone and fax number of the newspaper or magazine you'd like to advertise in from *British Rate and Data*. Commonly known as *BRAD*, this is a monthly publication which lists full details of media in the UK. A copy should be available for reference purposes in your local library.

Contact the advertisement department for a rate card. This will provide information concerning the publication area, readership (perhaps in terms of the type and number of readers) advertisement rates and deadlines for insertion. Having studied this, you should telephone or preferably visit the newspaper or magazine to discuss the type, size, contents and appearance of the recruitment advertisements that you want (see Chapter 3).

A selection of rate cards for local and national newspapers plus a trade magazine are reproduced in Figures 2.3–2.7, by courtesy of the East Anglian Daily Times Company Ltd, Express Newspapers Plc and Turret Group Plc.

Radio

With an ever-expanding number of stations catering for local and special interests, the radio is becoming an increasingly popular regional advertising medium. Many radio stations broadcast special jobfinder advertisements throughout the day for companies looking for new recruits.

Advertising for employees through the radio has many advantages. Your advertisements will be transmitted over a wide geographical area to a potentially large audience. With a mix of music, local news and information, chat shows and 'phone-ins, a variety of age groups listen, thus making it a suitable medium for different types and levels of jobs. Advertisements can also be broadcast very quickly, sometimes within hours. If they sound stylish and polished – always rely on in-house experts to create them – they will enhance a professional company image among all listeners, job seekers *and* customers.

Nevertheless, there are several disadvantages that must be considered carefully. Some people have the radio on as background noise while they are working, tidying the home or driving to the office. It rarely has their full attention and concentration. Even when it does, few have tuned in to hear advertisements and their thoughts will invariably wander when they're on, or they may start station hopping to find more music.

The radio is also a transient medium. An advertisement lasts for perhaps 30 seconds, which is a very short period in which to put across all the important points, and is then finished. It is usually difficult to remember the details given (What was that company's name? What was its 'phone number?) Most listeners will not have a pen and pad handy to make notes.

In comparison with other local sources of recruitment, such as free job centres, the radio is quite expensive, and will probably not provide noticeably better results. A 30-second advertisement on a small local radio station could cost from £10 to £25 plus VAT, depending on the station's transmission area and audience size (these are approximate 1991 figures). A series of 18 advertisements over a three-day period – possibly the minimum number needed to obtain sufficient exposure – would therefore cost £180 to £450 plus VAT.

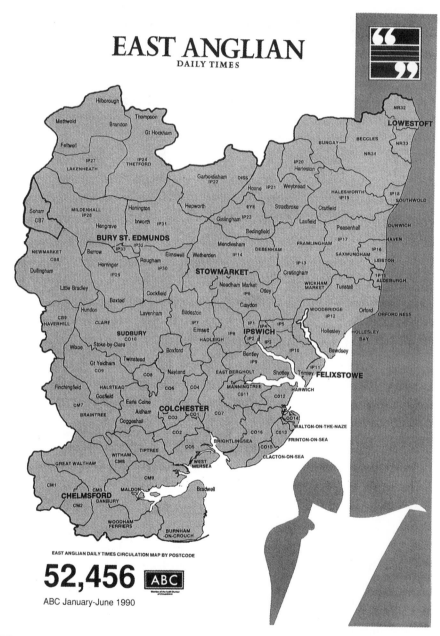

Figure 2.3   **A local newspaper's rate card**

EAST ANGLIAN 52,456
DAILY TIMES
ABC January-June 1990

ADVERTISEMENT RATES - All prices excluding VAT

RUN OF PAPER

ROP £5.25
(per single column centimetre - minimum 3 centimetres)
Full Page £1323.00
Half Page £661.50
Special Position (guaranteed) ....15% surcharge
(Front page and title corner - details on application)
Financial Reports £8.48
Colour ROP or Classified (minimum size 10 x 2)
Single Spot ....25% surcharge
Multi Spot ....Prices on application
Full Process ....Prices on application

CLASSIFIED advertisements are published in the East Anglian Daily Times and Evening Star

CLASSIFIED

Recruitment (display or semi) £10.54
Motors £7.12
Property £7.12
Other Classifications (display or semi) £8.64
Public Notices £8.99
Auctions £6.57
Lineage (minimum 3 lines)
    Private and Trade £1.71
    Recruitment £1.99
Box Numbers (fixed charge) Lineage ....Plus 4 lines
Box Numbers (fixed charge) Display £4.49
Personal Announcements Lineage ....£1.24 per line
Personal Announcements Display £3.36

DEADLINES	MECHANICAL DATA	COLUMN WIDTHS (mm)		
ROP and Classified order and copy: 48 hours prior i.e. Monday for Wednesday et seq.	Column length 360 mm; screen 35 per cm. 7 columns per page display, 8 columns per page classified. Production - Photosetting, artwork, bromides or original photographs required. Blocks or mats not acceptable. Printed web offset. Studio design and artwork services available at no extra charge. Ad format "B".	Columns	Display (7 cols. per page)	Classified (8 cols. per page)
		1	36	31
		2	75	65
		3	115	100
		4	154	134
		5	194	168
		6	233	203
		7	273	237
		8	–	272

POST CODE BREAKDOWN OF CIRCULATION AREA

Postal District (Sector)	Location	Households 1981	Postal District (Sector)	Location	Households 1981	Postal District (Sector)	Location	Households 1981
CB7 (5)	Soham	4,224	CO10 (8)	Clare	1,878	IP15	Leiston	1,192
CB8	Newmarket	10,400	CO10 (0,6,7,9)	Sudbury	11,729	IP16	Leiston	2,326
CB9 (0,8,9)	Haverhill	5,433	CO11	Manningtree	3,626	IP17 (1,2)	Saxmundham	2,685
CB9 (7)	Haverhill Rural	2,143	CO12	Harwich	7,071	IP17 (3)	Leiston	789
CM1	Chelmsford	19,012	CO13	Frinton-on-Sea	4,153	IP18 (6)	Southwold	1,851
CM2	Chelmsford	16,790	CO14	Frinton-on-Sea	1,920	IP19	Halesworth	3,396
CM3 (1,2,3)	Gt. Waltham	4,238	CO15	Clacton	15,892	IP20	Harleston	2,179
CM3 (4)	Danbury, Essex	3,091	CO16	Clacton Rural	4,940	IP21 (4)	Diss	2,159
CM3 (5)	Woodham Ferrers	3,272	IP1	Ipswich	13,385	IP21 (5)	Harleston	1,460
CM3 (6)	Burnham Rural	2,495	IP2	Ipswich	10,366	IP22	Diss	5,700
CM7	Braintree Rural	15,293	IP3	Ipswich	9,699	IP23 (7,8)	Eye	1,852
CM8	Witham	9,647	IP4	Ipswich	11,620	IP24	Thetford	7,656
CM9 (6,7)	Maldon, Essex	6,085	IP5	Ipswich Rural	2,754	IP26 (4,5)	Swaffham	2,917
CM9 (8)	Tiptree	2,895	IP6 (8)	Stowmarket	1,848	IP27 (0)	Thetford	3,264
CO1	Colchester	3,512	IP6 (0,9)	Ipswich Rural	2,633	IP27 (9)	Lakenheath	2,905
CO2 (0) ·	Colchester Rural	1,516	IP7	Hadleigh	4,271	IP28 (6)	Bury St. Edmunds Rural	1,682
CO2 (7,8,9)	Colchester	8,989	IP8	Ipswich Rural	3,199	IP28 (7,8)	Mildenhall	4,900
CO3	Colchester	8,492	IP9	Ipswich Rural	3,765	IP29	Bury St. Edmunds Rural	2,825
CO4 (3,4)	Colchester	7,276	IP10	Ipswich Rural	2,381	IP30	Bury St. Edmunds Rural	3,704
CO4 (5)	Colchester Rural	2,405	IP11	Felixstowe	8,030	IP31	Bury St. Edmunds Rural	5,607
CO5 (7)	Colchester Rural	1,353	IP12	Woodbridge	6,872	IP32	Bury St. Edmunds	3,173
CO6 (1,2,3,4)	Colchester Rural	8,523	IP13 (0,6)	Wickham Market	2,624	IP33	Bury St. Edmunds	8,072
CO7 (7,8,9)	Colchester Rural	6,311	IP13 (7,8,9)	Framlingham	2,903	NR33	Lowestoft Rural	11,746
CO8 (5)	Colchester Rural	727	IP14 (1,2,3,4,5)	Stowmarket	8,533	NR34	Beccles	7,062
CO9 (OPCS)	Halstead Rural	7,642	IP14 (6)	Debenham	1,157			400,115

East Anglian Daily Times
HEAD OFFICE
Press House
30 Lower Brook Street, Ipswich IP4 1AN.
Tel: 0473 230023. Telex: 98172.
Fax: 0473 232529.
Classified Ads: 0473 233233.

BRANCH OFFICES	Telephone
BURY ST. EDMUNDS, Lloyds Bank Chambers, Buttermarket	702588
COLCHESTER, 6 Culver Street West	571251
FELIXSTOWE, 120 Hamilton Road	284109
HALESWORTH, 16 Thoroughfare	2202
LEISTON, 72 High Street	830472
LOWESTOFT, 147 London Road North	65141
STOWMARKET, 1 Market Place	674428 & 674429
SUDBURY, 1 King Street	71297
WOODBRIDGE, Barton House, 84 The Thoroughfare	385353

Rates effective from September 10, 1990

ADVERTISING AGENCIES CONTACT:

AMRA Advertising Media Representation Agency Ltd.
London: 242 Vauxhall Bridge Road, London SW1V 1AU. Tel. 071-828 7141. Fax. 071-828 6685
Manchester: Byrom House, Quay Street, Manchester M3 3HG. Tel. 061 834 2050. Fax. 061 835 2781

Figure 2.3 *concluded*

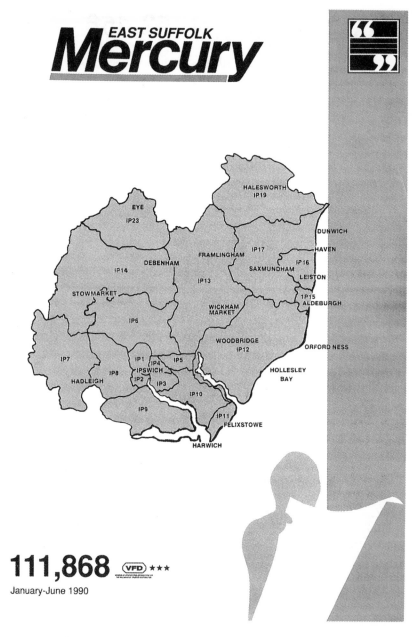

Figure 2.4   A local newspaper's rate card

111,868
 ★★★

January-June 1990

ADVERTISEMENT RATES - All prices excluding VAT

RUN OF PAPER

ROP Full Series £4.84
(per single column centimetre - minimum 3 centimetres)
Full Page £1219.68
Half Page £609.84
Special Position (guaranteed) ....25% surcharge
(Front page details on application)
Colour ROP or Classified (minimum size 20 x 3)
Single Spot ....25% surcharge
Multi Spot ....prices on application
Full Process ....prices on application

EDITIONS
Edition rates available on request.

CLASSIFIED
FULL SERIES
Recruitment £11.07
Motors £3.85
Property £3.85
Other Classifications £4.48
Public Notices £5.44
Lineage (minimum 3 lines) Private and Trade
  Recruitment £2.67
  Motors £2.24
  Property £2.24
  Others £1.40
  Box Numbers £5.56

DEADLINES
ROP:
Monday for Thursday
CLASSIFIED:
Monday for Thursday
Recruitment – Tues. for Thurs.
Motors – Tues. for Thurs.
Property – Tues. for Thurs.

MECHANICAL DATA
Column length 360 mm; screen 35 per cm. 7 columns per page display, 8 columns per page classified. Production - Photosetting, artwork, bromides or original photographs required. Blocks or mats not acceptable. Printed web offset. Studio design and artwork services available at no extra charge. Ad format "B".

COLUMN WIDTHS (mm)

Columns	Display (7 cols. per page)	Classified (8 cols. per page)
1	36	31
2	75	65
3	115	100
4	154	134
5	194	168
6	233	203
7	273	237
8	–	272

POST CODE BREAKDOWN OF DISTRIBUTION AREA

IP1 1,2,3,4,5,6	IP7 5 Hadleigh	Wherstead	Eyke RAF Bentwaters	IP13 6 Bredfield	Onehouse Wetherden	Friston Knodishall
IP2 0,9	Upper Layham IP7 6	IP9 2 Bentley	Sudbourne Tunstall	Grundisburgh Hasketon	IP14 4 Bacton	Saxmundham Snape
IP3 0,8,9	Elmsett Kersey	Capel St Mary Chelmondiston	Tunstall Common	Little Bealings Lower Ufford	Cotton Finningham	IP17 2 Bruisyard
IP4 1,2,3,4,5	Whatfield IP7 7	Holbrook Stutton	IP12 3 Alderton	Ufford IP13 7	Old Newton IP14 5	Peasenhall Sibton
IP5 7	Bildeston	IP10 0 Bucklesham	Bawdsey Boyton	Bedfield Brandeston	Earl Stonham Mendlesham	IP17 3 Darsham
Kesgrave Martlesham	Chelsworth Hitcham	Falkenham Kirton	Hollesley Rendlesham	Charsfield Earl Soham	Mickfield Stowupland	Dunwich Middleton
Rushmere IP6 0	Wattisham IP8 3	Nacton Trimley St. Martin	Air Base Shottisham	Kettleburgh IP13 8	Wetheringsett IP14 6	Minsmere Westleton
Barham Claydon	Belstead Burstall	Trimley St. Mary IP11 7	Sutton	Dennington IP13 9	Ashfield Debenham	Yoxford IP19 0
Great Blakenham Henley	Chattisham Copdock	Felixstowe Orwell Green	IP12 4 Newbourne Waldringfield	Framlingham Parham	Helmingham Stonham Aspal	Halesworth IP19 8
IP6 8 Barking	Hintlesham Sproughton	IP11 8 Felixstowe	IP13 0 Campsea Ashe	IP14 1 Stowmarket	IP15 5 Aldeburgh	Holton IP19 9
Creeting St Mary Needham Market	Washbrook IP8 4	Walton IP11 9	Easton Hacheston	IP14 2 Battisford	IP16 4 Aldringham	Blyford Bramfield
IP6 9 Coddenham Green	Bramford Little Blakenham	Felixstowe IP12 1	Little Glemham Marlesford	Combs IP14 3	Leiston Theberton	Wenhaston
Crowfield Otley	IP9 1 Shotley	Melton Woodbridge	Parklands Pettistree	Buxhall Great Finborough	Thorpeness IP17 1	
Playford Westerfield	Shotley Gate Tattingstone	IP12 2 Bromeswell	Wickham Market	Haughley	Farnham	

East Suffolk Mercury

HEAD OFFICE
Press House
30 Lower Brook Street, Ipswich IP4 1AN.
Tel: 0473 230023. Telex: 98172.
Fax: 0473 232529.
Classified Ads: 0473 233233.

BRANCH OFFICES	Telephone
BURY ST. EDMUNDS, Lloyds Bank Chambers, Buttermarket	702588
COLCHESTER, 6 Culver Street West	571251
FELIXSTOWE, 120 Hamilton Road	284109
HALESWORTH, 16 Thoroughfare	2202
LEISTON, 72 High Street	830472
LOWESTOFT, 147 London Road North	65141
STOWMARKET, 1 Market Place	674428 & 674429
SUDBURY, 1 King Street	71297
WOODBRIDGE, Barton House, 84 The Thoroughfare	385353

Rates effective from September 10, 1990

Figure 2.4 *concluded*

Figure 2.5   **A local newspaper's rate card**

Evening Star

33,837

ABC January-June 1990

ADVERTISEMENT RATES - All prices excluding VAT

RUN OF PAPER

ROP	£4.62
(per single column centimetre · minimum 3 centimetres)	
Full Page	£1164.24
Half Page	£582.12
Special Position (guaranteed)	15% surcharge
(Front page and title corner · details on application)	
Financial Reports	£7.72
Colour ROP or Classified (minimum size 10 x 2)	
Single Spot	25% surcharge
Multi Spot	prices on application
Full Process	prices on application

CLASSIFIED advertisements are published in the East Anglian Daily Times and Evening Star

CLASSIFIED

Recruitment (display or semi)	£10.54
Motors	£7.12
Property	£7.12
Other Classifications (display or semi)	£8.64
Public Notices	£8.99
Auctions	£6.57
Lineage (minimum 3 lines)	
Private and Trade	£1.71
Recruitment	£1.99
Box Numbers (fixed charge) Lineage	Plus 4 lines
Box Numbers (fixed charge) Display	£4.49
Personal Announcements Lineage	£1.24 per line
Personal Announcements Display	£3.36

DEADLINES

ROP and
Classified order
and copy:
48 hours prior
i.e. Monday
for Wednesday
et seq.

MECHANICAL DATA

Column length 360 mm; screen 35 per cm.
7 columns per page display,
8 columns per page classified.
Production - Photosetting, artwork,
bromides or original photographs required.
Blocks or mats not acceptable.
Printed web offset.
Studio design and artwork services
available at no extra charge.
Ad format "B".

COLUMN WIDTHS (mm)

Columns	Display (7 cols. per page)	Classified (8 cols. per page)
1	36	31
2	75	65
3	115	100
4	154	134
5	194	168
6	233	203
7	273	237
8	–	272

POST CODE BREAKDOWN OF CIRCULATION AREA

Postal District (Sector)	Location	Households 1981	Postal District (Sector)	Location	Households 1981	Postal District (Sector)	Location	Households 1981
C07 (6)	East Bergholt	2.117	IP6 (0,9)	Ipswich Rural	2.633	IP13 (0,6)	Wickham Market	2.624
C010 (6)	Sudbury	3.460	IP6 (8)	Stowmarket	1.848	IP13 (7,8,9)	Framlingham	2.903
C011 (1)	Manningtree	1.835	IP7	Hadleigh	4.271	IP14 (1,2,3,4,5)	Stowmarket	8.533
IP1	Ipswich	13.385	IP8	Ipswich Rural	3.199	IP14 (6)	Debenham	1.157
IP2	Ipswich	10.366	IP9	Ipswich Rural	3.765	IP16 (4)	Leiston	2.326
IP3	Ipswich	9.699	IP10	Ipswich Rural	2.381	IP30 (9)	Bury St. Edmunds Rural	2.246
IP4	Ipswich	11.620	IP11	Felixstowe	8.030	IP33	Bury St. Edmunds	1.222
IP5	Ipswich Rural	2.754	IP12	Woodbridge	6.872			109,246

(OPCS)

Evening Star

HEAD OFFICE
Press House
30 Lower Brook Street, Ipswich IP4 1AN.
Tel: 0473 230023. Telex: 98172.
Fax: 0473 232529.
Classified Ads: 0473 233233.

BRANCH OFFICES

	Telephone
BURY ST. EDMUNDS, Lloyds Bank Chambers, Buttermarket	702588
COLCHESTER, 6 Culver Street West	571251
FELIXSTOWE, 120 Hamilton Road	284109
HALESWORTH, 16 Thoroughfare	2202
LEISTON, 72 High Street	830472
LOWESTOFT, 147 London Road North	65141
STOWMARKET, 1 Market Place	674428 & 674429
SUDBURY, 1 King Street	71297
WOODBRIDGE, Barton House, 84 The Thoroughfare	385353

Rates effective from September 10, 1990

ADVERTISING AGENCIES CONTACT:

AMRA Advertising Media Representation Agency Ltd.
London: 242 Vauxhall Bridge Road, London SW1V 1AU. Tel. 071-828 7141. Fax. 071-828 6685
Manchester: Byrom House, Quay Street, Manchester M3 3HG. Tel. 061 834 2050. Fax. 061 835 2781

Figure 2.5 *concluded*

Daily Express	FULL DISPLAY (S.C.C.)	SEMI-DISPLAY (S.C.C.)	LINEAGE (PER LINE)
——————————— RECRUITMENT ———————————			
EMPLOYMENT PLUS LONDON & SE (Tuesdays only)	£20.00	—	£4.00
NATIONAL (Wednesday & Thursday)	£77.00	£72.00	£14.00
SOUTHERN EDITION (Wednesday & Thursday)	£64.00	£58.00	£11.00
NORTHERN & SCOTTISH EDITION (Wednesday & Thursday)	£45.00	£41.00	£9.00
——————————— LEISURE ———————————			
U.K. NATIONAL (Saturday)	£54.00	£46.00	£9.50
NORTHERN & SCOTTISH EDITION (Wednesday)	£38.00	—	£7.00
OVERSEAS NATIONAL (Saturday)	£59.00	£55.00	£11.00
NORTHERN & SCOTTISH EDITION (Wednesday)	£40.00	—	£8.00
——————————— PROPERTY ———————————			
NATIONAL (Tuesday & Friday)	£54.00	£48.00	£10.00
SOUTHERN EDITION (Tuesday & Friday)	£42.00	—	—
NORTHERN & SCOTTISH EDITION (Tuesday & Friday)	£34.00	—	—
——————————— BUSINESS OPPORTUNITIES ———————————			
NATIONAL ONLY (Monday only)	£64.00	£58.00	£12.00

DAILY STAR

	FULL DISPLAY (S.C.C.)	SEMI-DISPLAY (S.C.C.)	LINEAGE (PER LINE)
——————————— ALL CATEGORIES ———————————			
NATIONAL	£35.00	£33.50	£6.00
SOUTHERN OR NORTHERN EDITION	£28.00	£26.00	£5.00

SUNDAY EXPRESS

	FULL DISPLAY (S.C.C.)	SEMI-DISPLAY (S.C.C.)	LINEAGE (PER LINE)
——————————— RECRUITMENT ———————————			
NATIONAL ONLY	£88.00	£80.00	£17.50
——————————— LEISURE ———————————			
NATIONAL ONLY	£80.00	£72.00	£16.00
——————————— PROPERTY ———————————			
NATIONAL ONLY	£80.00	£72.00	£16.00
——————————— BUSINESS OPPORTUNITIES ———————————			
NATIONAL ONLY	£77.00	£72.00	£16.00

ALL RATES SUBJECT TO V.A.T.

Figure 2.6   A national newspaper's rate card

Add on the expense of in-house advertisement production at around £30 to £40 plus VAT.

If you're thinking of advertising on the radio, you should talk to business colleagues and acquaintances who have used it to see how effective they found it. Should you be sure it is worthwhile, approach your local radio station. Ask for a rate card explaining its transmission area, actual and potential audience and the various advertisement packages on offer. Then outline your ideas to their advertisement executives. Be guided by their advice and expertise, ultimately depending on their experience to produce a successful recruitment advertisement for you. (Although more relevant to written advertisements, see Chapter 3).

A radio rate card is reproduced in Figure 2.8, by courtesy of Suffolk Group Radio Plc.

Television

You can advertise on a regional or national basis through the Oracle Teletext Service on ITV and Channel 4. With over six million homes in the UK owning a teletext television set, a huge audience, far in excess of the press or radio, is available to you. Viewers can study your recruitment advertisement(s) at their leisure, with plenty of time to note down all of the key points (See Planning adverts, page 61). Recruiting staff through the television is still widely regarded as a new and innovative approach. Companies which use this medium may therefore be seen as go-ahead and dynamic.

The costs involved have to be taken into account, however. Prices vary from £550 to £1500 plus VAT for a half-page advertisement on screen for three months in one particular television region (Grampian, Granada, Thames/London Weekend Television and so on). Lengthier contracts – for six and twelve months – include a discount of approximately 17.5 and 35.0 per cent respectively. To advertise across all regions, the price is £5750 plus VAT for a half-page advertisement over three months rising to £9450 and £14 850 plus VAT for six- and twelve-month agreements. (These are 1990–91 figures.)

Thus, this medium may not be your immediate choice if you are seeking to fill just one vacancy, although shorter and less expensive one month contracts could be negotiable and worth considering. Should you regularly recruit staff – perhaps you rely on temporary employees to meet fluctuating, seasonal demands – then it might be worthwhile approaching other users to see how successful it is for

Nursery Trader, established since 1874, is the only independently audited magazine to reflect the rapidly expanding market for child and nursery products both in the UK and abroad.

As the birth rate has climbed so has the number of buyers who want to read Nursery Trader — we are therefore pleased to confirm a 1989 ABC (Audit Bureau of Circulation) figure of 3,202 (an increase of 707 copies) with a print run of 4,000 per month which ensures total coverage of a growing industry both at home and abroad: Ten per cent of our circulation now goes to key buyers abroad. Nursery Trader, published monthly, caters for all buyers — from the hard-core of independents to department store groups and mail order companies — a readership which is constantly monitored and updated by detailed research into the market that we know and understand.

Editorially, our experienced team writes with authority — Nursery Trader is the official journal of the British Association of Pram and Nursery Retailers — and, in addition to first class coverage of the UK market, will be keeping abreast of developments in Europe: to this end we will be publishing the second issue of our "EUROPEAN SUPPLEMENT" in August.

Other Nursery Trader publications that must feature prominently on your schedule include daily newspapers at the Autumn Child and Nursery Fair, Spring Pram and Nursery Fair as well as the annual Nursery Trader Directory, a complete reference guide to the Nursery trade.

Thanks to our all round experience, and exclusive editorial features we know that Nursery Trader is being read by the people that make the major buying decisions in the modern nursery world.

Figure 2.7   A trade magazine's rate card

RATES
and
DATA

* Effective January 1991

1991 Editorial Features List

January	Toy Fair Preview
	On The Move
February	Junior Fashion Fair Show Preview
	The Co-Ordinated Nursery
March*	Harrogate Pram & Nursery Fair
	Preview
April	Harrogate Fair Review
	Pushchairs
May	Cots/Mattresses
June	Safety Supplement
July	Sit 'n' Rides & Push-Alongs
	Prams & Combinations
August	Junior Fashion Fair Preview
	Soft Toys
	European Supplement
September*	Child & Nursery Fair Preview
October	Child & Nursery Fair Review
	Cologne & Paris Review
November	Dallas Review
	Feeding Equipment
December	Nursery Furniture
	Annual News Round-up
	Annual Directory

*Please note that the NURSERY TRADER 'Daily News' will be published and distributed at both the Harrogate 'Pram & Nursery Fair' and the Earls Court 'Child & Nursery Fair'.

ABC Audit Bureau of Circulation figure of 3,202.
1990 Print Run 4,000.
The **only** independently certified circulation of any Nursery Journal.

NURSERY TRADER

Rates per insertion	1	3	6	12
Full Page (Full Colour)	£826	£792	£757	£722
Full Page (Mono)	£514	£479	£445	£408
Half Page (Full Colour)	£653	£618	£584	£547
Half Page (Mono)	£350	£315	£281	£244
Quarter Page (Full Colour)	£547	£513	£479	£443
Quarter Page (Mono)	£244	£210	£176	£140

Colour — Spot Colour:	£109
Full Colour:	Rates are excluding separations if required
Special Positions:	Facing matter £85 extra subject to availability
Inserts:	Accepted by arrangement
Bleed Pages:	£55 extra
Cancellation:	6 weeks prior to publication
Classified Corner: (Sits Vac, Business For Sale/Wanted, Agents Required)	£10.00 per single column centimetre
Buyers Guide:	Headings of your choice with name and address of company plus logo if required £168 per year for twelve issues.

All advertisements are accepted subject to the standard conditions of Turret Group plc

MECHANICAL DATA

Full Page (Bleed)	303 x 216mm
Full Page (Trim)	297 x 210mm
Full Page (Type Area)	267 x 184mm
Half Page	130 x 184mm or 267 x 89mm
Quarter Page	60 x 184mm or 130 x 89mm
Printing Process	Sheet fed litho
Copy Requirement	Right reading emulsion down positives Screen — colour 133/54m. Mono 48m.

Figure 2.7 *concluded*

them. Contact Oracle Teletext Ltd for a rate card and to discuss precise requirements (See Appendix C).

A rate card is reproduced in Figure 2.9, by courtesy of Oracle Teletext Ltd.

Making choices

Having looked at the various internal and external sources of recruitment – and having asked yourself whether they will reach the right people in the right numbers at the right price – you must decide which one(s) to select. These further questions may help you to make the correct choice:

- What type and level of job do you have to fill?
- What kind of person do you wish to apply for the job?
- Where are these potential applicants?
- Are there present employees who could do the job well?
- If so, what sources are available to you within the company?
- If not, which external sources can you use?
- Which sources will possible applicants see (or hear)?
- Are you operating on a limited budget?
- Will the likely costs be in proportion to the importance of the job?
- Which sources have you or your colleagues used before?
- Were they successful or unsuccessful?

Whatever sources of recruitment are finally chosen, you must measure and assess the response to each of them. Only then will you be able to deduce whether or not you have picked the right ones. If not, changes should be made for future recruitment programmes (see Monitoring results, page 70).

Summary

Question   Where can staff be recruited from?
Answer   Many present employees will be able enough to be transferred or promoted to fill vacancies as and when they arise, especially if you've been recruiting in accordance with a manpower plan. Alternatively, you'll need to look outside the company.

Jobfinder Rate Card

Based on seven advertisements per day, broadcast between 0530 and 0100.

	ORWELL		SAXON		GROUP	
	Commercial Rate		Commercial Rate		Commercial Rate	
Two days	£273.00	£19.50	£161.00	£11.50	£392.00	£28.00
Three days	£409.50	£19.50	£241.50	£11.50	£588.00	£28.00
Three-Ten days	Multiples of:	£18.00	Multiples of:	£10.00	Multiples of:	£25.00
Ten days or more	Multiples of:	£15.50	Multiples of:	£ 9.00	Multiples of:	£22.00

Commercial production including the "Jobfinder", and single in-house voice **£35.00**

THE ABOVE PRICES ARE FOR COMMERCIALS THIRTY SECONDS DURATION
ALTERNATIVE DURATIONS AVAILABLE –

10 Seconds — 50%   20 Seconds — 20%   40 Seconds + 30%
50 Seconds + 65%   60 Seconds + 80%

Cancellation of Overnight Packages can only be accepted in writing not less than 28 days before the start of broadcast – cancellation during a campaign will be reinvoiced at the appropriate rate relative to the number of commercials already broadcast

Effective 1st AUGUST 1989
VAT NOT INCLUDED

IPSWICH SALES OFFICE - ELECTRIC HOUSE - (0473) 216971
BURY ST EDMUNDS SALES OFFICE - LONG BRACKLAND - (0284) 701511

Figure 2.8   A local radio station's rate card

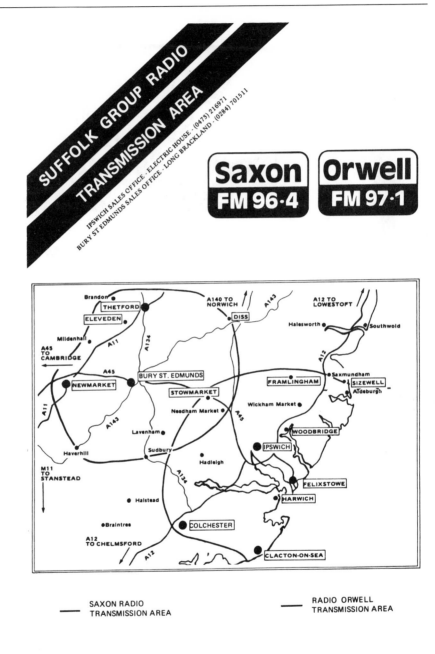

Figure 2.8   *continued*

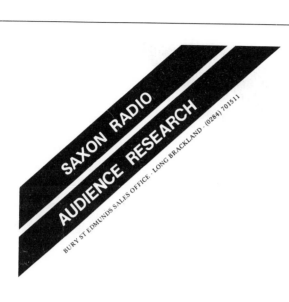

CATEGORY	% REACH SAXON SURVEY AREA	AUDIENCE
ALL ADULTS 15+	31%	74,000
15 - 24	22%	8,000
25 - 34	27%	10,000
35 - 44	43%	20,000
45 - 64	34%	22,000
65+	23%	14,000
ABC 1's	27%	19,000
C2DE's	32%	55,000
CIC2's	38%	38,000
MALE	31%	39,000
FEMALE	30%	35,000
FEMALE WITH CHILD (HOUSEWIVES)	42%	22,000

AUDIENCE CALCULATIONS BASED ON 4 WEEK'S LISTENING RESEARCH
NOVEMBER 1987 - RSGB/HALLETT ARENDT

Figure 2.8 *continued*

CATEGORY	% REACH ORWELL SURVEY AREA	AUDIENCE
ALL ADULTS 15+	41%	191,000
15 - 24	32%	18,000.
25 - 34	33%	29,000
35 - 44	55%	42,000
45 - 64	43%	52,000
65+	40%	50,000
ABC 1's	31%	57,000
C2DE's	48%	134,000
CIC2's	44%	111,000
MALE	43%	95,000
FEMALE	39%	96,000
FEMALE WITH CHILD (HOUSEWIVES)	40%	39,000

AUDIENCE CALCULATIONS BASED ON 4 WEEK'S LISTENING RESEARCH
NOVEMBER 1987/HALLETT ARENDT

Figure 2.8   *continued*

POPULATION - ADULTS 15+ = 610,000

CATEGORY	% REACH	AUDIENCE
ALL ADULTS 15+	40%	244,000
15 - 24	31%	23,000
25 - 34	33%	37,000
35 - 44	52%	58,000
45 - 64	41%	68,000
65+	38%	58,000
ABC 1's	31%	71,000
C2DE's	44%	173,000
CIC2's	44%	140,000
MALE	42%	119,000
FEMALE	38%	125,000
FEMALE WITH CHILD (HOUSEWIVES)	43%	60,000

AUDIENCE CALCULATIONS BASED ON 4 WEEK'S LISTENING RESEARCH
NOVEMBER 1987 - RSGB/HALLETT ARENDT

Figure 2.8 *concluded*

ITV ORACLE C4

REGIONAL CLASSIFIED...REGIONAL CLASSIFIED...REGIONAL CLASSIFIED

Regional Classified Advertising
Rate Card 4
Effective July 1, 1990

	FULL PAGE			½ PAGE		
	Standard Rate	Series Discount 17.5% (Approx) 35.0%		Standard Rate	Series Discount 17.5% (Approx) 35.0%	
	3 months	6 months	12 months	3 months	6 months	12 months
THAMES/LWT	2,750	4,500	7,150	1,500	2,500	3,950
CENTRAL	2,050	3,350	5,250	1,150	1,850	2,850
GRANADA	2,050	3,350	5,250	1,150	1,850	2,850
TVS	2,050	3,350	5,250	1,150	1,850	2,850
YTV	2,050	3,350	5,250	1,150	1,850	2,850
ANGLIA	1,450	2,400	3,750	800	1,350	2,050
HTV	1,450	2,400	3,750	800	1,350	2,050
STV	1,450	2,400	3,750	800	1,350	2,050
TYNE TEES & BORDER	1,450	2,400	3,750	800	1,350	2,050
ULSTER	1,450	2,400	3,750	800	1,350	2,050
TSW	1,000	1,700	2,650	550	950	1,450
GRAMPIAN	1,000	1,700	2,650	550	950	1,450
NATIONAL	10,400	17,150	27,050	5,750	9,450	14,850

NOTES:

1. This ratecard supersedes all previous Oracle Regional Classified ratecards.
2. Refer to Oracle Display Ratecard for national and regional display advertising rates.
3. See over for Terms & Conditions.
4. Check with your representative for advertisement booking and regulations.
5. Discounts on annual contracts will be reflected in quarters 3 and 4. See 7d overleaf.
6. All prices are subject to V.A.T.

Figure 2.9   An Oracle Teletext rate card

Question   How should a source of recruitment be assessed?
Answer   When studying a particular source, you must always ask yourself, 'Will it put me in touch with the right type of people in the right numbers at the right price?' If the answer is positive, consider proceeding with it.

Question   Which internal sources of recruitment are most commonly used?
Answer   Personal recommendations, noticeboards, newsletters and memoranda are popular ways of contacting potential applicants among your existing workforce. They all have advantages and disadvantages, though, and ought to be studied carefully to see which are appropriate for your individual circumstances.

Question   What external sources of recruitment are available?
Answer   Choose from among 'word of mouth', notices, job centres, private agencies and consultants, educational institutions, careers centres, the press, radio and television. Each has its own benefits and drawbacks which need to be thought about.

3 Attracting applicants

Once you have selected a source of recruitment which will put you in contact with the right type and number of people at the right price, you should spend time planning the contents and designing an appropriate style and layout for your job advertisement. Also, you ought to monitor and subsequently evaluate the results of your recruitment advertising campaign so you can make any necessary changes for the future.

Planning adverts

The main aim of any job advertisement must be to encourage a compact pool of suitable applicants to apply for the job. It should further discourage unsuitable applicants from getting in touch, and mutually wasting time and resources. Basing all recruitment advertisements on the job description and employee specification will ensure that everyone knows exactly what is involved with the post and whom you wish to employ. Thus, the most appropriate people (That's the job for me . . . I'm just what they're looking for!) will contact you. Inappropriate ones (I don't fancy doing that for a living . . . I'm not what they want anyway) will choose not to.

Although the contents of all job advertisements will vary according to the individual job description and employee specification, there are some ingredients that should be common to each of them. Bearing

61

in mind the constraints of a particular source of recruitment – for example, you may be short of room on a job centre or employment agency noticeboard – you'd usually try to supply as much information as possible about:

- the job title
- the location
- the duties
- the salary
- the fringe benefits
- the company
- the person required
- how to apply.

The job title

Taken from the job description, this must be clear and precise. Steer away from generalized titles. Replace 'Driver' with 'Articulated Lorry Driver'. Avoid in-house titles too. Change 'Refuse Operative' to the easily understood 'Floor Sweeper'. Make sure the job title given is in no way misleading. Often, it will be used as the heading of an advertisement. If it is unclear, job seekers may wrongly assume the post is unsuitable for them and will not read on.

The location

Tell potentially interested applicants exactly where-the job will be based. Always be specific. If advertising locally, put 'Allenby Industrial Estate' rather than 'Ipswich'. Should you be advertising nationally, state 'Penrith' instead of 'Cumbria'. Some people might not be able or want to work on the Allenby Industrial Estate or in Penrith; thus you'll reduce the number of unsuitable applications received.

The duties

Describe the job – its purpose, position in the organization, main tasks and responsibilities – as fully as space will allow. You must ensure that applicants know precisely what they'll have to do. Convey a totally honest and realistic picture of the job, with its good *and* bad features, even if you think it could dissuade some people from applying. It's far better that they drop out now rather than later in the recruitment process, when you'll have spent time and money on reading their applications, interviewing and testing them; or after recruiting them, as you'll then have to begin looking for a new employee all over again.

For example, a nursery store owner might detail a shop assistant's job as follows: 'Responsible to the proprietor, the successful candidate will be expected to sell baby clothes and nursery equipment to the general public. Other duties will include unloading, unpacking and displaying stock deliveries from suppliers, keeping the shop clean and tidy and running errands as required'.

The salary

State either an exact salary or, if you have room to negotiate, a possible range making certain the scale is in line with what your other employees earn in the same or similar jobs. Avoid vague statements simply describing the undisclosed salary as 'first-rate', 'highly attractive' or 'competitive'. Everyone defines such phrases differently.

As an example, applicants earning £10 000 and £30 000 per annum may all apply for a job with an unstated £20 000 salary labelled as 'first-class', as they interpret the comment in relation to their own present level of income. Clearly, those on £10 000 are likely to be unsuitable and those on £30 000 uninterested when they discover the actual sum involved. Much time and effort could have been avoided, and a large pool of applicants reduced, if '£20 000' had been mentioned to begin with.

The fringe benefits

Nowadays, fringe benefits such as luncheon vouchers, discounts on company goods, low interest-rate loans and free medical insurance are an integral part of an employee's financial package in an increasing number of jobs at all levels. In these days of well documented demographic changes, skills shortages and so forth, you will need to detail these attractive benefits as clearly and prominently as the salary.

Perhaps a company needing to recruit a new sales manager may put: 'We offer generous fringe benefits including 30 days' holiday per annum, a non-contributory pension scheme, free health screening and family BUPA and life assurance equal to four times the annual salary'.

The company

Describe your company as fully as you can so that people can decide if this is the type of organization they want to work for and will wish to employ them. You may choose to comment on such information as the company's activities, number of divisions and employees, products and services, customers and market share, sales turnover and growth plus plans for the future. Ideally, you'll highlight those areas most appropriate to the job and the type of people likely to apply for it. Would-be accountancy staff will be interested in financial data, sales employees in products, customers and so on.

A hotel advertising for chamber staff, carefully sidestepping a potentially sexist reference to 'chambermaids', could state 'A small family-run hotel, we have six single and eight double or twin bedrooms all with en-suite bath and shower, central heating, colour television, radio and tea- and coffee-making facilities. Four of our double bedrooms also have an extra lounge area. We cater mainly for business residents attending conferences and exhibitions in nearby Harrogate'.

The person required

Listing all the essential requirements, and as many desirable ones as possible, will encourage people to assess carefully their chances of success before applying for the job. (Am I over 18? Have I a full, clean driving licence? and so on.) Effectively, you're asking a potential applicant to screen themselves, thus saving you the time and trouble of weeding out wholly unsuitable applications. The more criteria you supply, the better your pool of applicants should be.

For example, an office manager seeking an office junior might say: 'To join our team, you must have a friendly and outgoing nature, be able to type at 50 words per minute and have 5 GCSEs (at C grade) or their equivalent, including Mathematics and English. Previous experience of office work would be an asset'.

How to apply

Everyone needs to be told who and where to apply to. Giving a full name and address, whether your own or an agency's, is far better than a box number as few people will submit personal, confidential information to an unknown source. Also state how and by when they should apply. Letters of application, with or without a curriculum vitae, application forms and telephone calls are the most common ways of screening and shortlisting candidates for interview (see Chapter 4). A closing date – perhaps for a month's time – may help to ensure a speedy, prompt response. Ask applicants to quote a reference number to help you measure the success of the advert/ source of recruitment (see Monitoring results, page 70).

An advertisement may thus conclude: 'Please send a handwritten letter of application with your curriculum vitae to Charlotte Hicks, Sanderson and Sons Ltd, Shotley Bridge Industrial Estate, Shotley Bridge, Yorkshire BR14 7XL. Your application should arrive no later than 28 March 1991. Please quote Ref.No NT11 in all correspondence'.

An example of a job advertisement in a newspaper is reproduced as Figure 3.1, by courtesy of Pentos Retailing Group Ltd.

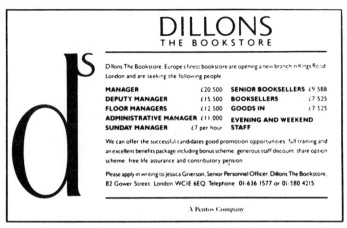

Figure 3.1   A newspaper advertisement

Designing adverts

Whether you're advertising internally (noticeboards, newsletters, memoranda) or externally (notices, agency noticeboards, the press), your job advertisements must be well designed. They should attract and then interest people so much that they read on and want to apply for the job. When drafting your recruitment advertisements, bear in mind the following points which are universally applicable. A job advertisement should be:

- eye-catching
- concise
- logical
- humour-free
- non-discriminatory

Eye-catching

You must ensure your recruitment advertisements demand attention even though committed job seekers will invariably peruse the entire noticeboard or newspaper page reading all advertisements including the drab and unenticing ones. There will be many other potentially suitable people who are simply looking to see what's happening in the employment market, who's seeking staff, how much is being paid and so on. If you can catch their eye, they may study the advertisement, subsequently applying for and perfectly filling the vacancy.

There are various ways of drawing attention to a job advertisement. Probably the easiest is to make it as large as you can. A big poster outside your premises or the largest advertisement on a magazine page is hard to miss. However, such a simple approach will not always be practical. You may have limited room available on a noticeboard or too small a budget allocated to press advertising. Thus, other methods should be thought about as well.

Wherever you advertise, have a bold heading. You can use the job title itself if it sounds impressive or is unusual (a 'What's my Line?' type job title will certainly be eye-catching). Alternatively, you might prefer to put the name of your company across the top of the advertisement. Do this if it is both well known *and* has a good reputation locally or nationally, as appropriate.

Artwork, worthy of a lengthy text in its own right, has a key role to play in making a recruitment advertisement appealing. An offbeat shape – see the excellent example in Figure 3.2 – will draw the eye to it. A thick black border will set it apart from the rest. An illustration, if appropriate to the job, or colour, if not too costly, may be worth considering. Different shades and styles of typeface are often used to good effect as well. Adopting a uniform house style for all future advertising offers the significant benefit of instant recognition among those looking at employment opportunities. However, make certain that the adopted style is adaptable for all types and levels of jobs and other advertising campaigns.

When planning artwork, spend some time scanning advertisements in the source(s) of recruitment you intend to use. Learn from them, seeing which are especially attractive and deciding why they are so appealing. Talk to local printers who can offer much helpful advice on style and layout. If advertising in newspapers and/or magazines, the art department will be well worth contacting too.

Examples of eye-catching advertisements – for various reasons –

Figure 3.2   A newspaper advertisement

Bettys TAYLORS Kings

CAREERS FAIR

MONDAY 8th MAY 1989

We have over 700 people working at our Tea & Coffee Factory, Bakeries, Bettys Café Tea Rooms, Bettys By Post and Head Office.

On Monday 8th May 7.00pm - 9.00pm we will be holding a Careers Fair in the Oak Room at Bettys York.
Staff and Managers from all areas of our business will be available to discuss a wide range of careers with you in:

Marketing . Engineering . Design . Accounting .
Administration . Trainee Management . Computing.
Baking . Confectionery . Manufacturing

We also have both Full and Part Time vacancies for the following positions:

Assistant Managers . YTS Trainees . Sales Assistants
Cashiers . Cooks . Kitchen Assistants . Waiters . Waitresses
Cleaners . Supervisors . Retail Manager
Assistant Executive Chefs . Assistant Executive Housekeeper

As a trainee you will have the opportunity to be sponsored for external training courses, including City & Guilds & HCTB Courses furthering your education.

If you would like to find out more about careers within the company, or are interested in any of the job vacancies listed above please call in for an informal chat on Monday 8th May anytime between 7.00pm - 9.00pm.

EVERYONE WELCOME

Figure 3.3 A recruitment poster

are reproduced as Figures 3.1–3.3 by courtesy of the Pentos Retailing Group Ltd, the Royal Mail and Betty's Café Tea Rooms Ltd.

Concise

Once the potential applicant has seen the recruitment advertisement, he must study it. To encourage this, the text should be brief and to the point. Supply key information as succinctly as possible. Use compact paragraphs and short sentences. Stick to plain English, avoiding fancy and confusing phrases. If details are not relevant, cut them out. Should your words not be absolutely clear, change them. Otherwise, the reader will lose interest and look at the next advertisement instead.

Logical

Similarly, set out the text in a sensible and progressive order (job duties, salary, fringe benefits and so on). Jumping back and forth to and from different subjects is discouraging. Each paragraph should deal with one, self contained topic. Every sentence should make one simple point. Do not cover the same topic or points again. Never repeat yourself.

Humour-free

Although humour can be very effective in some advertising campaigns, steer clear of it in recruitment advertisements. Most people view job hunting as a serious matter – they could be unemployed with a mortgage to pay and children to support – and might be alienated by comments which they regard as flippant or patronizing. Also, everyone's sense of humour is different. 'Funny ha-ha' to one person may be 'funny peculiar' to another.

Non-discriminatory

As always, you should avoid discriminating on the grounds of sex, marital status or race. The presentation and phrasing of your advertisements must not imply that only people of a particular sex, marital status or racial group should apply for the job.

Be especially careful of your job title. Replace the discriminatory 'Barmaid' or 'Salesman' with 'Bar Person' and 'Sales Person'. For jobs traditionally done by one sex or another in the past, make it obvious that you invite applications from both sexes. Put 'Typist (Male or Female)' and 'Car Mechanic (Male or Female)'. Should you use a personal pronoun, state 'He/She' or 'He or She'. The Equal Opportunities

Commission and the Commission for Racial Equality can advise on more specific circumstances (see Appendix C).

It is worth adding here that you should encourage suitable people with disabilities to contact you too. Perhaps add a phrase such as 'We welcome applications from disabled persons'. This will help to ensure that you are seen as a company which offers fair and equal opportunities to *all* suitably qualified applicants.

See Appendices A and B for more information on how to avoid discriminating during the recruitment and selection process.

Monitoring results

Attracting a pool of potentially suitable applicants is a cornerstone of a successful recruitment policy, from which a shortlist of candidates can be drawn up and the right person subsequently chosen for the job. You cannot afford to leave its success to chance and good fortune. Selecting appropriate sources of recruitment and creating attractive advertisements is also a time-consuming and costly matter. You must be certain that your time and money are well spent.

Therefore it is sensible to measure and assess these early stages of the recruitment process so that any necessary changes may be implemented for the future. Start by drawing up a simple analysis form with the job title/company department as the heading. Down the left, note the sources of recruitment used and their respective costs. Across the top, add columns showing the number of 'Initial enquiries', 'Applications received', 'Unsuitable applications' (those immediately rejected) and 'Suitable applications' (those invited for interview).

Initially, you'll be looking to see which sources produce a compact number of appropriate applicants and few (if any) inappropriate ones at an acceptable cost. This should be easy to judge either by putting a reference number on each job advertisement and telling applicants to quote it in communications or by adding the question 'Where did you learn of this vacancy?' to an application form. Costs per reply (suitable *and* unsuitable) can be calculated by dividing the total financial outlay by the respective numbers.

Make a careful note of enquiries, applications submitted and so forth on a daily basis, filling out the analysis form once this stage of the recruitment process has been completed. Naturally, it will take some considerable time to build up a comprehensive and accurate picture of which sources of recruitment are best for you, especially if you recruit staff for various types of jobs at different levels. Avoid making rash decisions based on only a few recruitment advertising campaigns.

Having assessed (and possibly changed) the sources of recruitment used, you can then set out to measure the success of different job advertisements. For each particular source, draft an analysis form with the same basic heading and columns as before. Down the side of the page, however, have a list of the various advertisements used, along with their costs.

By slightly varying aspects of your recruitment advertisements and then registering the response to each, you can see which produce the best results. Regularly making minor adjustments to timing, location, size, contents and so on enables you to gather so much knowledge, over a lengthy period of time, that you'll be able to design much improved advertisements for the future.

Summary

Question   What is the main aim of a recruitment advertisement?
Answer   It has a dual purpose: namely to encourage suitable people to apply whilst discouraging unsuitable ones. It is hoped that only a compact pool of potentially suitable applicants will actually contact you.

Question   How can this dual aim be achieved?
Answer   A well designed advertisement will attract and retain the interest of prospective applicants. Carefully phrased contents will then enable them to decide if they are suitable for the company and job (and vice versa).

Question   What information should be included in a recruitment advertisement?
Answer   Every job advertisement must be based on the job description and employee specification. Subject to the constraints of the individual source used, try to provide details about the job's title, location, duties, salary and fringe benefits. Refer to the company itself, the type of person required and how to apply for the job.

Question   How should a recruitment advertisement be designed?
Answer   There are five basic rules to follow. It needs to be eye-catching, concise, logical, humour-free and non-discriminatory.

Question   How can the success of a recruitment advertising campaign be assessed?

Answer   A reference number should be attached to each advertisement with applicants being asked to quote it in all communications. In this way, you should be able to monitor the number of suitable and unsuitable people applying per source of recruitment and/or advertisement.

4 Screening applicants

Once you have attracted an appropriate number of potentially suitable applicants at a reasonable cost, you'll want to whittle them down to a shortlist of candidates to be interviewed and tested for the job. The various methods used to screen applicants – by letter, curriculum vitae, telephone and application form – have to be considered. You must also decide how to handle applications, inviting suitable applicants to an interview and rejecting unsuitable ones in a fair and proper manner.

Choosing a screening method

You'll probably have a fairly lengthy list of applicants from which to select a new employee. Ideally, you'd interview all of them so that the best person is less likely to slip through the net. However, with perhaps 100 applicants or more to choose from, the time (at least 30 minutes or so per interview) and costs (your time, their travel expenses and so on) involved will usually make this an impractical approach.

Screening applicants by letter with or without a CV, telephone or application form allows you relatively quickly and inexpensively to compare them with the employee specification and each other. Outstanding applicants can be asked to come in to meet you and the remaining ones promptly eliminated. Normally, you'll be expecting to interview perhaps six to eight candidates who most closely match your employee specification. It may be a good idea to extend this conveniently sized shortlist if you have many existing employees applying and want to maintain staff morale and work relations – or at least take rejected internal applicants to one side to carefully explain your reasons for turning them down.

Before studying the main screening methods, consider the guidelines for choosing the right ones. Answering these questions may help you to reach the correct decision:

- What qualities do I want to assess?
- How would applicants most like to apply?
- How much time do I have?
- Which is the most cost-effective approach?

What qualities do I want to assess?

Check the essential and desirable requirements – and contra-indications too. Ask yourself which screening method will best enable you to evaluate them swiftly and accurately. Often, it will be obvious which one you should select. If you're trying to recruit a new telephone sales person, you'll naturally ask applicants to 'phone so you can hear how they speak, handle a conversation and so on. Should you be looking for a storekeeper who will have continually to fill out forms when working, you'd possibly prefer to use an application form to see how well he completes it.

How would applicants most like to apply?

Consider how various types of applicants, such as youngsters, racial groups and senior executives, would react to each of the four screening methods available. School and college leavers, often inexperienced and nervous, may not yet be capable of chatting freely on the telephone. Racial groups could be unable to fill out an application form unaided and, incidentally, should not be eliminated because of this unless personally completing it is a valid test of the standard of English needed to do the job effectively. Senior executives might be impatient with application forms, preferring the informality of a 'phone call.

How much time do I have?

Calculate how long you have to fill the vacancy and the speed with which the various screening methods allow you to complete this stage of the recruitment process, whilst still retaining accuracy. The telephone will probably provide the most immediate response as applicants may automatically reach for it as they finish reading the advertisement. Letters, curricula vitae and application forms, which have to be applied for, sent out, carefully read, completed and returned, could take much longer. Of course, you may not be in a hurry at all. Selecting a new employee is an important decision which should not be rushed.

Which is the most cost-effective approach?

Obviously, the expense in terms of money and the time involved should be taken into consideration when making a choice. The telephone, letters and curricula vitae are possibly less costly than application forms which need to be carefully designed, produced, distributed and so forth. Nevertheless, you may feel that the added expense is of secondary importance to getting the right person for the job.

Bear these four questions in mind, especially the first two, when looking at the different methods of screening applicants available to you.

Letters and curricula vitae

Many companies ask applicants to send a letter of application, with or without a curriculum vitae. Such an approach appears to have several advantages. On its own a typed or handwritten letter may be useful if you wish to assess an applicant's typing or writing ability, assuming he was not assisted in its completion. These may be important criteria for the job. Also, nearly everyone is familiar with writing letters and should find it easy to compile one. It could further save you the time involved with drawing up and sending out application forms or being ready for 'phone conversations at all hours.

Unfortunately, letters of application have significant disadvantages. The main and largely insurmountable problem is that the applicant is free to include and exclude whatever he wants. Although a precisely worded advertisement stating exact requirements can help, he is still unlikely to put in all the facts you wish to check. Those that are referred to will be in no particular order. It will take time to read, find and extract what information there is. Also, some applicants will be better at letter writing than others. This doesn't necessarily mean they'll be better at the job.

Asking applicants to attach a curriculum vitae to their letter should ensure that key facts are placed within a more structured and logical format, such as Personal Details, Education, Work Experience and Leisure Interests. You'll now find it easier to spot the details you seek. A CV can also be used as the basis of an interview plan, see Devising an interview plan, page 94.

However, it is still up to each individual applicant to decide what he mentions and, more importantly, prefers to overlook. If a fact is omitted, you do not know if this is a simple oversight or a deliberate act. A further difficulty may arise because some applicants, perhaps racial groups, might not be fully familiar with curricula vitae and how they should be drawn up. Potentially suitable applicants could thus appear wholly unsuitable.

Using the telephone

Talking on the telephone is a prompt way of screening applicants, especially appropriate if good speech and the ability to chat informally are necessary attributes for the job. Information can be swiftly collected and assessed with suitable applicants being invited for an interview. Follow a verbal invitation with written confirmation (see Selecting and rejecting applicants, page 85). Cutting back on paperwork, by removing the necessity of drafting, posting and reading completed application forms (or letters and curricula vitae), is an added bonus.

However, be conscious of the limitations of this screening method. Some interested, and possibly suitable, applicants may simply be too shy to telephone you. Others could find it difficult, particularly if they're already in employment. Putting a 'phone number in a job advertisement will also increase the number of casual, half-interested enquiries. The sheer volume of superfluous calls throughout the day can make this a time-consuming, costly approach. If you're inexperienced, you may further find it hard to assess the real person behind the voice. Rejecting applicants, and running the risk of offending them or becoming involved in an argument, is a worry too.

If you choose this method, and it is appropriate in some circumstances, you'll need to try to overcome these drawbacks. List the precise qualities required in advertisements, stressing that only people who meet all of them should apply (see Planning adverts, page 61). Make sure you, or a colleague assigned to carry out screening on your behalf, have sufficient time set aside to handle calls.

Have an answering machine switched on out of office hours so that applicants who are unable to telephone during the day may leave their name and a 'phone number where they can be called back the next evening. Draw up a list of questions to put to applicants which will establish whether or not they match the employee specification (see Devising an interview plan, page 94). If you cannot face rejecting over the telephone, because some applicants can become quite upset and demanding, say you'll be in touch (you might say you have others to consider before a decision can be made) and then send a rejection letter (see Selecting and rejecting applicants, page 85).

Application forms

Probably the best way of screening applicants is to ask them to fill out an application form. There are many valid reasons for adopting this approach. Full details about the job and your company can be sent with the form. Recruitment is a two-way process in which both employer *and* employee select each other, and every applicant wants to know all about the work and the company he may be employed by. Only then can he decide if he wishes to proceed with his application, attend an interview and accept a job offer.

Supplying background information is in your interests too. Some people, realizing that this isn't the job or company for them, will not apply. This will save you the time and money incurred in handling a large number of applications. It will also reduce the likelihood of the successful candidate starting work with misapprehensions about what's involved. The recruitment process is sometimes unsuccessful because the new employee discovers too late that the job is not as he imagined. He then begins to arrive late for work, becomes disruptive, takes days off and eventually resigns (or needs to be dismissed). Subsequently, the time-consuming and expensive search for a replacement has to start again.

With applicants answering the same questions in exactly the same place, it will be simple to check whether essential and desirable requirements are met. Some basic criteria – age, possession of a full driving licence and so on – can be quickly referred to and unsuitable applicants promptly eliminated, although more detailed requirements, perhaps relating to previous training, will need to be scrutinized carefully. You will be able to compare applicants directly and more easily. Application forms may also be used as the basis of an interview (see Devising an interview plan, page 94), with many interviewers dealing with each section of the application form in turn.

Of course, the main benefit of using an application form as a screening method – the simplicity of checking and comparing information – can only be derived if the form is well designed. Asking the right questions in the right order to elicit answers which enable you to match the applicant with the employee specification is difficult. There are several points that need to be thought about before an application form is drawn up.

Ideally, the form should be individually designed for the particular job, and composed after a careful study of the appropriate job description and employee specification. Perhaps school leavers would be asked more questions about their education than work experience (which may be limited). For potential managers, for whom school could be a distant memory, questions would concentrate on recent work history. However, drafting a separate form for every job is often impractical, and many large companies devise three standard ones: for junior, senior and other appointments.

An application form must be short and concise if applicants are to be encouraged to fill it out. Only relevant and easily understood questions should be included. At the same time, plenty of room must be given for the applicant's answers. Trying to compress ten years' work experience into a thumbnail-sized space is as discouraging as a lengthy list of irrelevant questions.

Every form should be set out in a logical and progressive manner. Although the precise content and order of all application forms will differ according to the job and company, most would include the following:

- opening instructions
- personal details
- education and training
- employment history
- medical information
- further details
- closing instructions
- interviewer's notes

Opening instructions

At the top of the form, tell the applicant how he is expected to fill it out. This can be done in his own hand or by typewriter, perhaps depending on what you're trying to assess. If copies of the application form need to be given to colleagues who may be involved in selecting candidates for a shortlist, request completion in black ink and block capitals which make a photocopy easy to read.

Other information typically supplied here would be under the headings 'Position applied for' and 'Where did you learn of this vacancy?' This question is especially useful as it enables you to monitor and evaluate the success or failure of the various sources of recruitment used (see Monitoring results, page 70).

Personal details

Simply ask the applicant to list his full name, address, a telephone number where he can be contacted and his date of birth. Unless absolutely relevant, do not request detailed personal information such as marital status, the number and ages of children and nationality. Not surprisingly, because these details are rarely related to the applicant's ability to do the job well, they will create the impression that you will use the answers to discriminate on the grounds of sex, marital status or race.

Education and training

Educational background can be set out in various ways, perhaps under the titles of 'General Education', 'Further Education' and 'Special Training'. Whatever the layout, you want to know the names and addresses of all schools, colleges and universities attended from the age of 11 along with the respective dates of attendance. Details of examinations sat, with dates and grades, and any subsequent, specialized training (apprenticeships, in-house courses and so on) should to be requested as well.

Employment history

Commencing with his present or most recent job, the applicant should provide information such as his employers' names and addresses, employment dates, job titles, duties and responsibilities, opening and closing salaries and reasons for leaving. You could also ask how much notice needs to be given to his current employer.

Medical information

You obviously wish to be sure that you will be taking on a person who is sufficiently fit and healthy to do the particular job properly, bearing in mind that the demands of each job may vary enormously. The questions you pose here will therefore depend on the nature of the job available. You may simply ask 'Have you suffered from any serious illness in the last five years? (if yes, please supply details)'. Alternatively, you could be more precise with 'Do you suffer or have you suffered from any of the following?' You must refer to your employee specification before deciding what to put.

Below this same heading, you should also put 'Do you have a disability which is relevant to this job application? (if so, please describe the disability)' and 'Are you registered as disabled with the job centre? (if yes, please supply your registration number)'. You should not be setting unnecessary medical or physical requirements which may eliminate potentially suitable disabled applicants.

It is sensible and encouraging to preface questions on health and disability with a statement that you welcome applications from suitable people with disabilities. Use the recommended phrase 'A disability or health problem does not preclude full consideration for the job and applications from suitable people with disabilities are welcome'.

Further details

Towards the end of the application form, you'll probably enquire about the applicant's leisure interests, if you feel these may be of relevance to the job. Ask whether he is a member of any clubs, societies or professional institutions. Checking to see if he holds any positions of responsibility can be worthwhile too.

Asking a question such as 'Why do you want this job?' or 'What skills, knowledge and experience will you offer to us?' can be most revealing. Applicants who really want the job – and it is not a good idea to recruit anyone without genuine enthusiasm for the job and company, however good they might otherwise be – will carefully and fully complete this section. Casual applicants, filling in many forms without thought or commitment, will invariably leave it blank because it takes too much time and effort to complete.

Ask for the names, addresses and occupations of two referees who can vouch for the applicant, information supplied and his suitability for the job. Personal referees, biased family and friends, should be forbidden. Teachers or lecturers may be accepted from youngsters if they know them well. Previous and current employers, who have

Application for employment with BOOTS THE CHEMISTS

PLEASE RETURN COMPLETED FORM TO:

TO BE COMPLETED IN APPLICANT'S
OWN HANDWRITING

CONFIDENTIAL

Position applied for	Source of application (name of journal, newspaper or other)

PERSONAL DETAILS

SURNAME Dr./Mr./Mrs./Miss/Ms	NAME BEFORE MARRIAGE	DATE OF BIRTH
		PLACE OF BIRTH
FORENAMES		MARITAL STATUS

FULL ADDRESS (for correspondence)	PERMANENT ADDRESS (if different)
TEL. No. DATES AT THIS ADDRESS	TEL. No. DATES AT THIS ADDRESS

Do you have any restrictions on geographical mobility and/or a strong preference for a particular location? If so give details:	Have you been employed by the Company before? If so give details, including dates

	Any dates when **not** available for interview	Date available for employment
	Do you hold a valid driving licence? YES / NO	Do you require a U.K. work permit? YES / NO

REFERENCES	1. Name Address Occupation	2. Name Address Occupation

REFERENCES WILL NOT BE TAKEN UP FROM YOUR PRESENT EMPLOYER UNTIL AFTER AN OFFER OF EMPLOYMENT HAS BEEN ACCEPTED

99-04-859

Figure 4.1 An application form

MEDICAL HISTORY: Complete all questions. Have you had any of the following conditions? Please underline where applicable.

Epilepsy, fits, blackouts or recurrent faints. Migraine (or recurrent headaches) or dizziness. Anxiety, depression or other mental illness. Asthma, hay-fever, or infantile eczema. Diabetes. Psoriasis, dermatitis or other skin disease. Bronchitis, tuberculosis or other chest disease. Heart attack or stroke. Rheumatism or any back condition. Dyslexia. Recurrent absence from work for any reason. Persistent ear or throat infection. Recurrent episodes of diarrhoea.

YES / NO

Have you ever had a serious illness or injury?

YES / NO

Have you been treated at hospital at any time?

YES / NO

What was the date and nature of this treatment?

Are you currently under treatment of any sort?

YES / NO

What is the nature of this treatment?

Do you suffer any disablement?   YES / NO

Are you on the Disabled Persons Register?

Registration Number

POSITIVE replies to any questions may necessitate a Medical Examination, or further medical enquiry.
In these cases engagement could only be made subject to a satisfactory result.
Failure to reach the Company's requirements for particular occupations does not necessarily imply impaired health or unsuitability for other occupations.

EDUCATION AND TRAINING

	NAME AND LOCATION	RESPONSIBLE POSITIONS HELD	DATES		EXAMINATIONS PASSED OR TO BE TAKEN (with grades and names of courses studied)
			FROM	TO	
SCHOOLS					
COLLEGES					
OTHER EDUCATION AND TRAINING					

Please give details of any other specialised training you have undertaken.

Membership/Grade of professional institutions.

Brief outline of interests, hobbies, activities.

Membership of societies and positions of responsibility.

Figure 4.1 *continued*

PREVIOUS EMPLOYMENT—most recent first (include any vacation employment during last 3 years)					
Name and Address of Employer	Position held	Salary	Dates		Reason for leaving
			From	To	

What notice are you required to give your present employer? ....

What relevant skills or experience do you feel make you suitable for this vacancy?	Please add any further information you may wish to give in support of this application. (Use separate sheet if necessary)
Have you ever been convicted of any offence before a Court of Law? YES / NO If so give details:	

I CERTIFY THAT THE INFORMATION DETAILED IS CORRECT.

Applicant's signature .... Date ....
False or withheld information may lead to the termination of your employment.

Figure 4.1 *continued*

INTERVIEWER'S NOTES

INTERVIEWER'S
SIGNATURE ....   DATE ....

STORE	DISTRICT	AREA	SALES TEAM	HOURS PER WEEK

REFERENCES		PERM/TEMP/YTS	F/T	MORNINGS	AFTERNOONS	EVENINGS
REQUESTED	RECEIVED					

DATE OF JOINING	N.I. NUMBER	MEDICAL REQUIRED	
			YES / NO

ANNUAL SALARY	TO BE INDUCTED BY	JOB TITLE AND JOB CODE

Figure 4.1   *concluded*

seen the applicant in a work environment, should be encouraged as referees (see Taking up references, page 151).

Closing instructions

Finally, state to whom, where and by what date the application form must be returned. Then add a declaration such as 'I declare that all information given is correct. I understand that any false statement may lead to immediate dismissal' asking the applicant to read, date and sign it. Although you'll obviously seek to check all facts (by looking at certificates and diplomas, asking probing questions and taking up references), oversights do sometimes occur and such a declaration may provide you with some protection against exaggeration and outright deceit.

Interviewer's notes

If, as is common practice, you intend to take the appropriate application form into the interview room, you should allow yourself space to make notes about the interviewee. If possible, leave the back page free for jotted comments and observations (see Last-minute preparations, page 95).

An example of a well designed and thorough application form is reproduced as Figure 4.1, by courtesy of The Boots Company Plc.

Selecting and rejecting applicants

Whether you have asked applicants to telephone or send in a letter, curriculum vitae or completed application form, you should adopt the same approach towards the screening process. All written applications should be acknowledged as and when they are received, thus promoting a friendly and caring company image which will appeal to would-be employees. Applicants may also be customers and, even if rejected for this job, could want to apply for future vacancies as they arise. Make certain they maintain a high opinion of you by being polite and courteous at all times. Figure 4.2 is an example of a letter of acknowledgement.

Compare the information supplied against the employee specification. This is the yardstick by which each and every applicant (internal or external, regardless of sex, marital status, race and so on) should be measured and assessed. You're aiming to shortlist for interviews, and perhaps tests, those applicants who meet all the 'essentials', as

Dear Mr Jones

Thank you for your application for the post of Office Assistant.

This is receiving our careful attention and we shall be contacting you again shortly.

Yours sincerely

Maureen Reynolds
Sales Manager

Figure 4.2   A letter of acknowledgement

many 'desirables' as possible and who have no 'contra-indications'. Group applications into three categories: 'potentially suitable', 'suitable' and 'unsuitable'.

Potentially suitable applicants – usually those whom you have not been able to evaluate fully because they sent in an incomplete letter or CV – may be asked to supply further data, perhaps by completing an application form. On receipt of this, you can then decide into which of the two remaining categories they should be put.

Suitable applicants – and bear in mind you probably won't want to interview more than six or so – should be invited to meet you at a mutually convenient date and time, thus maintaining that pleasant and amiable company image. Perhaps telephone each applicant to discuss when they are free to come (unless they are currently employed, in which case your 'phone call could be embarrassing). Alternatively, write and ask them to contact you so that an interview can be arranged.

Once the interview has been set up, confirm full details of the date, time and exact location in writing. Explain how long it will last and who will be involved as well as supplying information about any tests that must be taken. Tell the applicant you will reimburse all reasonable travelling expenses and indicate how these should be reclaimed (perhaps a secretary can settle them on arrival when they may be more modest than after he has been interviewed and expects to be

Dear Mr Jones

Following our telephone conversation this morning, I write to confirm that you are invited to an interview at 10.30am on 16 May at the above address. Please report to reception.

Your interview should last for approximately 30 minutes and will be conducted by myself, Mr Rajesh Munglani, our assistant sales manager, and Mrs Jane Donovan, our office supervisor.

I enclose a map of Bradwell on which I have highlighted the location of our company. I have also sent you a copy of our annual report and a job description which you may find interesting.

Please bring your GCSE certificates to the interview. Finally, reasonable travel expenses will be reimbursed by our receptionist on arrival.

I look forward to meeting you next week.

Yours sincerely

Maureen Reynolds
Sales Manager

Figure 4.3   An invitation to an interview

rejected!). Ask him to bring certificates to be checked too. An example of a letter inviting a candidate to an interview is given in Figure 4.3.

With your letter, attach a map showing the location of your business premises so the candidate can find you easily. If appropriate, also include test guides and samples to show him what to expect. Most important of all, send a job description and company literature (if you have not already done so) so he can learn everything about the post and your organization.

Unsuitable applicants need to be rejected as quickly as possible, so that hopes are not unnecessarily raised. Rejection should also be done as pleasantly as you can. Avoid stating a reason for rejection,

---

Dear Mr Kimble

Thank you for your application for the post of Office Assistant.

After careful consideration, we regret to have to inform you that you have not been successful on this occasion.

However, we would like to thank you for your interest in our company and wish you well for the future.

With all good wishes,

Yours sincerely

Maureen Reynolds
Sales Manager

Figure 4.4   A letter of rejection

as applicants may contact you again and ask for further information, trying to get you to change your mind. Keep all rejected applicants' details for three months. This is the time during which they can appeal to an industrial tribunal because of alleged discrimination. Your records should show that you have acted properly. An example of a rejection letter is given in Figure 4.4.

Summary

Question   How can a large pool of applicants be reduced to a shortlist of candidates?
Answer   By asking applicants to send in a letter of application (with or without a curriculum vitae), telephone or complete an application form. This will help you to assess whether they are likely to be suitable for the job.

Question   Which screening method should be chosen?
Answer   It depends mainly on the qualities you want to evaluate and

how potential applicants would wish to apply. Bear in mind the time and expense involved with each of the four methods.

Question   How should an application form be designed?
Answer   It should be based as closely as possible upon the job description and employee specification and be short, concise and logical. Contents may include headings such as opening instructions, personal details, education and training, employment history, medical information, further details and closing instructions. Leave room for interviewer's notes as well.

Question   How should applications be processed and dealt with?
Answer   All applications must be acknowledged. They should then be compared with the employee specification and divided into three piles: 'potentially suitable', 'suitable' and 'unsuitable'. The first group should be asked to provide more information, the second invited for interviews and tests and the third rejected in a prompt and pleasant manner.

5 Interviewing candidates

Every selection interview is or should be a two-way process. You want to discover whether the candidate matches the employee specification closely and seems likely to be able to do the job well. He is trying to find out if this is the type of post he wants at a company he would like to work for. To exchange the necessary information successfully so that the most suitable person is chosen and will accept your job offer, you must prepare for interviews thoroughly. You need to be able to open, run and close an interview properly. You should know how to reach a final decision about each of the shortlisted candidates interviewed.

Making plans

Prepare for interviewing success by thinking about the type of interviews that should be conducted and when and where they ought to be held. Get ready for each particular interview by putting together a plan to follow and gathering up all the documents you need to take into the interviewing room with you.

Types of interview

A 'one-to-one' interview involves one interviewer and one interviewee talking to each other. Probably the most common type of interview, it appears to have much to offer. It is usually simple to agree on a place and a time to meet which suits the two people concerned. It is also a relatively informal affair. An experienced interviewer should be able to relax the candidate quickly, putting him at ease and establishing a rapport so that he chats freely about himself.

However, a 'one-to-one' interview – or individual interview as it is otherwise known – can be a most unreliable method of assessment. If this is the case, it is the fault of the interviewer who is typically inexperienced, unprepared and even biased against certain candidates, perhaps because of their sex, marital status or race. No manager should be expected to handle an interview alone without first having read widely on the subject (see Appendix D), been through extensive training (see Appendix C), and sat in on many other interviews to gain as much 'hands-on' experience as possible. If such simple steps are not taken, it will hardly be surprising if the wrong person is subsequently selected with all the potential problems (poor work performance, conduct and so on) that can ensue.

A 'panel' interview consists of two or more interviewers meeting each candidate to discuss his job application. Usually, between three and six interviewers would make up the panel – or board as it sometimes is called – perhaps including the department manager, the direct supervisor and an expert in the work, who can talk with authority about the job and question the candidate about his previous work experience.

The benefits of a panel interview are that collective experience and decision making increase the chances of the best person being chosen for the position. Panel members can also share the responsibility of asking questions, with each one specializing in their particular area of expertise. The others listen carefully to the answers and make notes which will help to remind them of each candidate after all the interviews have been completed. Having a panel further allows all departments likely to be involved with the successful candidate to be represented and have a say in his selection. Would-be interviewers can also be included to give them valuable experience, perhaps for future 'one-to-one' interviews.

Nevertheless, there are drawbacks that need to be considered and overcome. It may be hard to get all the panel members and candidates together at the same time, so timetables must be carefully planned and scheduled well in advance. Bear in mind that it can also be costly and time-consuming. Friction and ill feeling may develop among the panel if one person tries to dominate, questions overlap and everyone tries to talk at the same time. Attention must therefore be given –

and full agreement reached beforehand – as to the composition of the panel, the division and order of topics and the ground rules for making a selection decision. An interviewee, especially if young and inexperienced, could find such a formal situation tense and intimidating. He may become inhibited, revealing little or no information about himself. Therefore efforts must be made to create a friendly atmosphere (see Starting an interview, page 96).

A *'sequential' interview* is one of a series of interviews with various interviewers taking it in turns to meet the candidate on a one-to-one basis. Normally each interview will focus on a particular topic or group of topics. Sequential interviews can combine the best features of a one-to-one interview (informality, a warm rapport) and a panel interview (more experience, shared responsibilities) as well as providing a more comprehensive, in-depth assessment of each candidate. Unfortunately they can sometimes incorporate their worst features too (individual bias, additional selection time and costs and so on) and a manager must therefore weigh up the pros and cons carefully before adopting this approach.

Timing and location

Usually, the date and time of an interview will be mutually agreed between you and the candidate. You should make an initial approach by telephone, if appropriate, or by letter, asking him when it would be convenient to call in and see you. This conveys the impression of a caring and amicable would-be employer. Never impose a time on a candidate just to fit him into your schedule. Not only might he be unable to attend but such a demand may appear rude and unreasonable.

Always allow plenty of time for each interview, so that you avoid having to watch the clock and rush such an important matter. Perhaps 30 minutes or so should be set aside for junior posts (New Youth Training, clerical, secretarial, for example) rising to possibly 75 or 90 minutes for more senior positions (sales executives, department managers and so on). If interviewing several candidates in succession, ensure that their interview times are well set apart with approximately 20-minute intervals between each. These gaps enable you to overrun slightly, gather your thoughts and make notes, have a snack (but don't eat in front of a candidate as it is ill mannered and distracting) or visit the loo.

The location of an interview plays a key role in its success or failure. Both you and the candidate must be able to concentrate on asking questions and assessing answers to decide if you are well matched. Choose a quiet office or room (remembering that the job centre can offer appropriate interviewing space if necessary) without external noise, such as heavy machinery in operation or lorries being unloaded, or potential interruptions. Tell colleagues not to disturb you, disconnect the telephone and so on.

Consider the layout of the room. You want to be able to concentrate totally, so remove all obvious distractions, for example, pull down the blind if the sun will be in his eyes, or change his chair if it is low and uncomfortable. You'd like the candidate to feel relaxed and at ease so he'll talk openly. Having a large desk between you can be daunting. Create an air of relaxed informality by sitting around a table for a panel interview (it's less like a firing squad) and having two easy chairs and a coffee table for a one-to-one interview.

There are other measures you can take to help the candidate relax. Think about the impression you create by the way you behave. If you appear tense and nervous (sweaty brow, clenched fists, jerky movements, stammered questions and so on) or seem rude and indifferent (fiddling with paper clips, staring out of the window while he's talking, interrupting him and so on), then the candidate will feel increasingly edgy. Put him at ease by keeping your body still and leaning slightly forward to show you're interested in what he has to say. Look at him regularly, smiling and nodding to encourage him to speak. Listen to him, picking up and developing his comments. Be prepared to lead the conversation if he falters, otherwise let him do most of the talking, so that you find out all you want to know.

Devising an interview plan

An interview plan should consist of a list of topics that you want to cover during an interview with a number of questions under each heading which will help you to match the candidate with the employee specification. Draw one up in collaboration with your colleagues before any interviews are conducted with shortlisted candidates. Having a skeletal plan in front of you at an interview reminds you to deal with all the main areas (if you're nervous you may overlook one or two), allows you to listen to the candidate's answers without thinking what to say next and enables you to return or move to another topic or question if he dries up, rambles on or even tries to take over the interview.

It is up to you which topics and questions to include. Some interviewers base their interview plan on their application form or the letters and curricula vitae received from candidates. They work through each section in turn, checking details, asking questions and dealing with queries as they arise. Other interviewers, mindful that they are trying to compare candidates with the imaginary employee required, use the employee specification itself, posing questions about the candidate's physical make-up, attainments and so on.

A typical interview plan, as expanded on in Questions and answers, page 98) might begin with a brief chat about the company and job, bearing in mind that an interview is a two-way process and every candidate will want to know as much as possible about these topics. Following this, information given in the application form, curriculum vitae or letter could be checked to ensure the candidate really does meet the criteria set. Moving on, questions might be asked about his education, work experience, outside interests, any anomalies apparent in his application, and ambitions. Then, he could be given the opportunity to ask any questions he has thought of. Whatever your choice, always be flexible in your approach. Every interview and interviewee is unique, so do not adhere rigidly to a set order of topics and questions when the interviewee may reveal more about himself if approached differently. Use the plan as a loose framework around which the interview is built.

Similarly, avoid noting down too many questions that must be asked. Only a handful of strictly relevant ones, to spark a discussion or compare the candidate with the employee specification, should be recorded under each heading. Attempting to plough through a long list of questions will restrict the flow of the conversation – and make the candidate feel as though he's being interrogated by a police investigator!

Last-minute preparations

Before each interview, read through your job analysis notes, job description, employee specification and interview plan again. You will then be ready to talk about the job and be reminded of the qualities you are looking for and the loose and flexible order of the interview. Take another look at the candidate's application form, letter or curriculum vitae. You can then see how closely he resembles the ideal employee and decide on the facts you wish to check and the anomalies you want to mention.

Take the interview plan, employee specification and candidate's application with you into the interview so that you can refer to them as and when necessary. Make notes about the candidate during the interview as you can't expect to remember everything about him afterwards. Out of courtesy, always ask him for permission before you start jotting down comments, although he'll probably be flattered that you're sufficiently interested in him to do so. When taking notes, try to be as brief as possible, to avoid breaking up a free flowing conversation, and think carefully about your timing. It can demoralize the candidate if you note negative information immediately, so wait a few minutes.

Some interviewers write notes on the employee specification or on the candidate's application form, letter or curriculum vitae. Others draw up an assessment form comprising the essential and desirable requirements looked for. Appropriate comments are made under each heading during the interview with marks (from 1 to 6) given afterwards. The candidate with the highest overall score is then usually offered the job. Should you choose this approach – and it can be helpful – look on it as an aid, rather than the answer, to decision making. Don't become over-dependent on a set of figures relating to qualities which vary in importance to each other and differ according to the day-to-day needs of the job.

Starting an interview

Try to put each candidate at ease and establish a rapport with him as soon as he enters your business premises. By the time the interview begins, he should then feel relaxed and be ready to answer your questions in a confident, open manner. If interviews are well spaced out and run to schedule, consider meeting him personally when he arrives. This will instantly create a caring image and make him feel good about you and your company.

Typically, a candidate will be early for his appointment, perhaps arriving while you are still interviewing the previous candidate. You should therefore ask a colleague or a member of staff to greet him on your behalf. If he is simply ignored, he will soon become increasingly edgy and nervous ('Have I come to the correct office? Am I too early? Is this the right day? Did she mean this Thursday or next Thursday?') In the wrong frame of mind for his interview, he might panic and walk out, and even if he stays, it will take you longer to calm him down.

Whoever is responsible for meeting a candidate should acknowledge his arrival with a ready smile. This will make him feel welcome.

Asking for his name and then using it will reassure him that he is expected ('Good morning, Mr . . .? Ah yes, Mr Jones, you've come in for your ten-thirty appointment with Mrs Reynolds. I'll tell her you're here') He should be shown to a comfortable chair and, as appropriate, offered a cup of tea and company brochures to read while waiting for you. Reimbursing travel expenses and checking qualifications could also be attended to now.

Always adhere to the agreed interview time. If he is left sitting there for a further five or ten minutes, as often happens, it may unnerve or annoy him. He will also assume you are either incompetent or, more likely, ill mannered. The interview will then start badly. You will find it hard to relax him and gain his confidence.

Come out of your office into the reception area to welcome the candidate. Do not expect him to find his own way to you through an unfamiliar building. Not only will this seem rude and uncaring but, if directions given are unclear and the premises are large, he might become lost or even disappear completely. Save time and potential embarrassment by fetching him in person.

When introducing yourself, smile warmly and make eye contact thus showing that you are pleased to see him and keen to hear what he has to say to you. Build on this by shaking hands and addressing him by his name ('Hallo, Mr Jones, I'm delighted to meet you. I'm Maureen Reynolds, the sales manager who'll be interviewing you. Would you like to come with me?') Chat pleasantly en route to the interview. Questions such as 'How long did it take to travel here?' and 'Have you had a good journey?' can help to start a conversation and set a relaxed mood.

On arriving at the interviewing room, guide the candidate towards his seat. This is especially important if the layout is informal and it is not obvious who sits where. Many interviewers would then offer him a drink or a sweet to put him at ease, but this is largely unnecessary if the conversation is developing well. Also, leaving him alone while you go to make a cup of tea or coffee can heighten tension. If a member of staff is sent to do it, his return may disrupt the interview later on. The nervous candidate could even knock a drink over or choke and splutter on a sweet. He might further be expected to answer a question at the precise moment he takes a mouthful of hot tea or bites into a sweet, which will embarrass him.

Move on instead to introducing your fellow panel members (if appropriate) and briefly outlining the topics you intend to cover during the interview. This will allow the candidate to become accustomed to you, your colleagues and his surroundings and to gather his thoughts together for the forthcoming questions. A light-hearted approach with a dash of humour is often fitting here. For example:

> Let me begin by introducing you to my colleagues and telling you about the interview. To my left is Mrs Donovan, our office supervisor, who'll be talking about the job in a few moments. To my immediate right is Mr Munglani, assistant sales manager. Between us, we'll be chatting to you about your education, work experience, hobbies and ambitions. Next to him is Mr Platek, looking very mysterious. Nothing to worry about there. He's just taken charge of our customer care department and is sitting in for experience. He'll be watching and making notes if that's okay with you . . . Thank you . . . The interview should last around twenty-five minutes or so. You'll then have the chance to ask us any questions . . . get your own back if we've been too tough! How does that sound? . . Fine, then lets make a start . . .

Never make a decision about any candidate in these first few minutes. Far too many interviewers brag that they can make an accurate assessment almost instantly. Often, the basis for this 'assessment' is extremely tenuous, if not downright illegal (Poor fellow has a sweaty handshake and bites his nails. Obviously an insecure bag of nerves who can't handle pressure! Close-set eyes, looks rather shifty and untrustworthy. Can't have him! Ginger hair, always quick-tempered and unreliable. No use to us! Doesn't shave her legs, must be one of these modern women. Bit too modern for this company!) Such thoughts, sadly far from uncommon, owe more to the interviewer's prejudice and bias than a systematic analysis of the facts.

Every candidate, regardless of sex, marital status, race, disability, age and so on, must be given a fair and equal hearing, asked similar questions that provide answers which enable the interviewer to compare them with the employee specification and be judged solely on their ability to do the job. A decision should not be made until after the interview has been completed, when all the relevant facts have been obtained and are available for study and comparison with those of the other candidates.

Questions and answers

Having set the scene for the candidate, you should then refer to your interview plan. Loosely follow its framework throughout the interview. Consider the following topics and subsequent questions:

- the company
- the job
- checking facts
- education
- work experience
- outside interests
- anomalies
- ambitions.

The company

You – or a colleague if you have chosen to conduct a panel interview – may begin by talking about your organization. Perhaps refer to some of these areas:

- its history
- its products and services
- its customers
- its competitors
- its future plans.

Always start with the company, even though the candidate will probably already know all he wants to know from literature sent out with the application form and his own research. You're familiar with the company and should find it easy to talk about it, thus easing your nerves. The candidate will feel safe and more able to relax, aware that he has a few more minutes to 'acclimatize' before the serious questioning begins.

Mention those areas likely to be of most interest to each particular candidate, such as products and customers to a potential sales representative. They will all want to be told of the company's future plans, so refer to anticipated developments as well. Avoid talking too much; see this as a brisk introduction to the main part of the interview.

The job

Talking about the organization should naturally lead on to the job. Base your comments on these headings:

- its key role
- its location
- superiors and subordinates
- main duties and responsibilities
- terms and conditions of employment
- the type of person needed
- future prospects.

Again, the candidate will be aware of what the job entails – or ought to be if you posted out appropriate details and he is interested enough to find out more. Nevertheless, mention it early on as it should further help to put you both at ease (as you know what to say and he doesn't have to answer probing questions yet) and will also ensure that he has a general view of what is involved. Try not to make it sound more important than it is or run it down (possibly because you have foolishly taken an instant liking or disliking to the candidate). Simply aim to convey a brief, accurate idea of the job. Specific, in-depth questions can be dealt with at the end of the interview (see Concluding an interview, page 107).

Checking facts

If you have not already done so, you will want to establish that the candidate really does meet those key criteria set out in the employee specification (now perhaps transferred to an interview assessment form). Typically, you might ask questions such as:

- Are you over 18 years old?
- When were you born?
- Do you have a full, clean driving licence?
- Have you brought it with you?
- What qualifications do you have?
- Can you show me your certificates?

Bear in mind that the candidate might embellish the facts – or even lie outright – to obtain work. You must therefore make certain that the important information given on his application form, letter or curriculum vitae is wholly correct. If possession of a clean driving licence, various qualifications (or their equivalents) and so on are considered necessary to do the job properly, then ask to see them now, if you have not already done so. Otherwise, you may offer him the job and not discover the truth until after he has started work, which wastes your time, effort and money if you have to begin the recruitment process once more.

Education

Education, qualifications and training will normally be discussed in depth at some stage. The following questions could be appropriate:

- What did you most enjoy doing at school?
- What did you least enjoy doing at school?
- Why did you decide to go to that university?
- What made you choose that particular degree course?
- To what would you attribute your success at university?
- How have you benefited from that training course?

Education will be the central topic of many interviews, especially with younger candidates who are still at, or who have recently left, school, college or university. Asking these questions – and being flexible enough to move into other areas according to the answers – should enable you to piece together an accurate picture of the candidate's personality, skills and abilities. Although an older person's formal education is less relevant (or even irrelevant) if it is in the distant past, questions about any recent training could still be asked, if it might have a bearing on ability to do the job.

Work experience

The candidate's work record to date, particularly his present or last job, should be fully examined. These questions may produce informative answers:

- What do you do in an average day?
- Which tasks do you find easy to do?
- Which tasks do you find difficult to do?
- Tell me about the type of problems you have to handle.
- How did you deal with that problem?
- What do you like about your job?
- What do you dislike about your job?
- Why do you want to leave?

All candidates – even youngsters who have only ever had a Saturday or summer job – must be encouraged to discuss the work they have done. It is especially useful if previous work experience of a similar nature is listed as essential or desirable on the employee specification/ assessment form. Comparisons with the job description can thus be made. Concentrate less on the basic information already well documented in his application (the job title, who he worked for, how long he held the job) and more on what was actually involved, his strengths and weaknesses and his reasons for leaving, which can be extremely revealing.

Outside interests

Leisure pursuits could be of relevance to the job. Suitable questions might include:

- How do you relax?
- What do you do in the evenings and at weekends?
- Tell me about your hobbies.
- Are you a member of any clubs?
- Do you belong to any societies?

These questions are useful for providing background information about the candidate which may help you to reach a decision. For example, you might feel that a sports equipment salesman ought to have a keen interest in playing sports to do the job really well. In addition, the questions can be used to encourage a slow-moving conversation to start flowing. Most people enjoy explaining and talking about their hobbies.

Anomalies

Should you have any queries arising from the application form, letter or curriculum vitae in front of you, don't forget to ask about them, for example:

- Can you tell me why you attended six schools in as many years?
- What did you do in the 18 months between your last two jobs?
- Why did you take a large drop in salary moving from your previous job to your present job?
- Why haven't you filled in the 'Reasons for Leaving' section of your application form?

Of course, there may be nothing suspicious in any of the anomalies you've spotted. The candidate could have simply overlooked a question or failed to add an explanation about any comments that were likely to arouse your curiosity. Always ask if you're unsure or in doubt about any aspect of his background. You may uncover facts that will affect your choice.

Ambitions

Often, you'll want to talk to the candidate about his hopes and expectations of the future. Typical questions are:

- Why do you want to join our firm?
- What do you expect to gain from the job?
- Where do you want to be in three years?
- How do you see your future career developing?

Naturally, you'll be hoping that the chosen candidate sees a long-term future for himself within your company; you don't want to spend time and resources on training him only to have him leave after a short period. Question him carefully in this area.

Whatever topics and questions are covered within your interview plan, you should consider the different ways that those questions can be phrased and how they affect the success of the interview. Questions can be grouped under the following headings:

- open
- closed
- limited
- hypothetical
- leading
- multiple
- discriminatory.

Open questions

Beginning with words such as 'why', 'how' and 'what', open questions encourage the candidate to talk at length. They will enable you to find out about his personality, views and feelings. Think how revealing the answers to the following examples could be:

- How do you feel about your career so far?
- Why did you leave your last job?
- Why have you applied for this post?
- What qualities are needed for this job?

- How would you describe yourself?
- What will your referees say about you?

It may not be a good idea to ask open questions early in the interview when the candidate, especially if he is an inexperienced interviewee, will probably not yet be ready to talk informally. Stumbling, hesitant replies and embarrassed silences will simply make him even more nervous. Wait until he appears to be relaxed before introducing them into the conversation. An appropriate moment may arise after you have described the company and job and have checked facts. From then on, ask them regularly so that you get to know the candidate well.

Closed questions

Closed questions need only a 'yes' or a 'no' reply. Imagine what a candidate might say in response to:

- Did you like your school?
- Were you a school prefect?
- Did you study chemistry at school?
- Was your last job interesting?
- Do you like football?
- Do you enjoy reading?

Such questions have their uses. Early on, they are helpful for verifying facts ('Is your Higher National Diploma the equivalent of a degree pass?') and for keeping a tongue-tied candidate talking. Later on, they can bring a rambling conversation back to the point ('So, do you like travelling then, Mr Jones?') and force an evasive candidate into giving a direct response ('Mr Jones . . . Were you dismissed?')

Try not to use this form of questioning too much. A self-assured candidate can always develop his answer to continue the conversation ('Yes, I did like my school. I was particularly fond of . . .') but a tense or less talkative one will not be able to. A dull, unrevealing exchange will be the result ('Yes . . . no, not really . . . Yes . . . no, not at all . . .'). It will take a long time, which will seem like an eternity, to obtain all the information you want.

Limited questions

Starting with 'who', 'when', 'where' and 'which', limited questions usually produce a short, limited answer. As examples:

- Who was your housemaster at school?
- Who ran that training course?
- When did you obtain your certificate?
- When did you join that company?
- Where was your job located?
- Where do you go rifle shooting?
- Which club do you belong to?
- Which type of rifle do you use?

Similar to closed questions, these can be used to establish facts and keep the conversation moving. The candidate should find them easy to handle – after all, he knows all the answers. Use them sparingly, though, as they will make the interview develop sluggishly. It is far better to re-phrase them by saying 'Tell me about your housemaster at school, that training course . . .' which will produce extra information for you, as well as making the conversation more pleasant and interesting.

Hypothetical questions
Hypothetical questions ask the candidate to place himself in a particular situation. He then has to say how he would react in the following circumstances:

- What would you do if a client complained that one of your junior staff had been rude to her?
- How would you handle a customer who demanded a refund on a product that had obviously not been looked after properly?
- What would be your response to an employee who was late for work?
- How would you cope with persistent, unauthorized absences from work?

These are worth asking because they will enable you to assess whether the candidate knows what he is supposed to do in various work situations. However, ensure that they are relevant to the job. Think about three or four problems that the new employee is likely to encounter on a regular basis and mention them during the interview.

Leading questions
Leading questions signal the answer that you are looking for. As examples:

- We're looking for an industrious person. Are you industrious?
- You do have enough experience for this job, don't you?
- Can you deal with the pressures involved with this post?
- You'd be happy to work overtime when necessary, wouldn't you?

Such questions are never worth asking because the candidate, unless he is particularly honest and naive, will simply tell you what you want to hear. It is far better to rephrase leading questions into open ones ('What are your strengths in relation to this job?', 'What has your previous work experience involved?' and so on).

Multiple questions
Multiple questions contain several questions all rolled up into one. Consider the following:

- Tell me what you did in your free time at college? Did you belong to any societies? Or did you prefer sports? Were you in any teams?
- Tell me all about your first job after leaving polytechnic. What was it? Was it enjoyable? What did you learn from it?
- I see from your application form that you enjoy playing hockey. Where do you play that? Is there a local club? Are you a member of it?

Individually, all these questions have a place in the interview, helping you to find out a little more about the candidate. Ask them separately; otherwise you will appear confused and bewildered, and the candidate may become mixed up, not knowing which one to answer first.

Discriminatory questions
However they're phrased, there are some questions which should be avoided as they create the impression that you are discriminating against the candidate on the grounds of sex, marital status or race. Do not ask questions such as:

- Do you think a woman could do this job well?
- Will you be able to cope with the men working for you?
- Are you planning to marry in the near future?
- What will you do if your husband is transferred away from the area?

- Are you likely to have a baby soon?
- What will you do if your children are sick?
- How do you think you'll get on with our white employees?
- What will our white employees think about you?
- Are you going to want long holidays to go back home to the West Indies?
- We've never had a Pakistani manager before. Why should we now employ you?
- As an Irishman, don't you think you'd be better suited to a manual job?

These questions will – quite rightly – be interpreted as treating a candidate less favourably because of their sex, marital status or race than another candidate in the same circumstances. Having been asked such questions, a rejected candidate may decide to pursue a claim of unlawful discrimination at an industrial tribunal – and would deserve to win. Avoid thinking of and asking such questions. Judge a candidate solely on his ability to do the job.

Concluding an interview

Once you have covered the topics and questions highlighted in your interview plan, you should be coming towards the end of the time set aside for the interview. With perhaps five to ten minutes or so remaining, you would normally give the candidate the opportunity to ask you questions ('Well, we seem to have discussed everything we wanted to deal with. Are there any questions you'd like to put to us, Mr Jones?').

He will probably have a number of queries, possibly developing from information given in the job advertisement, company brochures and/or the interview. Typically, he might ask you to tell him more about various terms and conditions, his precise role and responsibilities within the department, company training schemes and his likely future with you. If your recruitment process has been thorough (analysing the job, drafting a job description and so on) and you have prepared for the interview well by reading job analysis notes, and so forth, you should be able to answer his questions fully.

Make sure that your answers are always scrupulously honest and realistic. Too many interviewers try to impress a potentially suitable candidate by just talking about the best features of the job and exaggerating how good it is ('Holidays? Oh, take them when you want, Mr Jones. We always like to accommodate our employees' needs'). Only when he starts work does the candidate discover the less pleasant aspects of the job and that the interviewer misled him ('Holidays? You can take them when you want so long as we're not left short-staffed. We have a staff rota system and I'm afraid that as you're the most junior you choose your holiday dates last'). A wholly fair and accurate impression of all aspects of the job and company must always be given if a newly recruited employee is not to become disillusioned and subsequently leave.

As soon as you have answered the candidate's questions, you should bring the interview to an end. Never make a job offer or reject a candidate at this stage even if he appears to match your employee specification precisely or seems totally unsuitable. In the heat of the moment it is far too easy to make a rash (and incorrect) decision based on feelings rather than facts. Wait until after all the interviews have been completed when you can make a cool and unbiased assessment of each candidate, compare notes about them and talk to your colleagues. This is the only way you can hope to reach a right and fair decision.

Rejecting a candidate there and then is not good practice. Even if your motive was to spare him the worry of not knowing, it will often still be regarded as a rude and heartless action ('Didn't give me much of a chance, did he? Just said I wasn't right for the job then threw me out!'). Ill feeling and resentment may be generated towards you and your company. ('Well, that's the last time I ever buy their goods and I'll make sure my friends don't go there either!'). Should you offer a reason for rejecting him, it could lead to a lengthy discussion or even a heated argument as he tries to persuade you to change your mind. The next, probably tense and nervous candidate will be kept waiting to see you.

It is far better to finish by simply thanking the candidate for coming to the interview and explaining what happens next ('Well, we seem to have covered everything then, Mr Jones. Many thanks indeed for coming along to see us. We'll be writing to you by the end of this week'). Sidestep any potentially embarrassing questions ('How did I do?' or 'What do you think your decision will be?') by standing up, smiling warmly at him and offering him a handshake. This will indicate the interview is now over. Show him out and bid him farewell.

Reaching decisions

Having interviewed all the shortlisted candidates, you then need to decide who should be offered the job. Reach a decision by carefully studying all the information you have gained about each candidate from their initial application (have you checked the key facts and dealt with anomalies?) and their interview (if important, how did you rate their appearance, speech and so on?) Compare this information with the essential and desirable requirements detailed on the employee specification or assessment form. Talk to other panel members and/or colleagues with whom the successful candidate will have to work. Agree on which candidate should be offered the job.

Sometimes, you will believe that none of the candidates could do the job well. Perhaps they do not fulfil all the essential criteria or possibly they have a contra-indication which became apparent during the interview. Consider the reasons for failing to find the right person. You may have set standards which are too high (are all the requirements really necessary?) or placed badly designed advertisement in the wrong media, thus attracting many unsuitable applicants. You might not have screened applicants fully, drawing up an inadequate application form or letting obviously unsuitable applications slip through. Then, you must decide whether to adjust your standards to fill the vacancy, bearing in mind that dropping requirements may not be prudent; or, alternatively to begin the recruitment process again using other sources of recruitment, advertisements and screening methods, asking yourself if you can afford to leave the job vacant any longer.

Hopefully, your recruitment methods to date will have been thorough and you will have three or four suitable candidates to choose from. Consider selecting the one who is most likely to be a good prospect in the long term, able enough to be promoted as other employees resign, are transferred or retire. If in doubt, do not hesitate to ask candidates to return for second interviews or to participate in various tests (see Chapter 6).

Once the selection decision has been made, you must offer the job to your first choice candidate, while holding one or two in reserve in case he turns you down if he is in demand. Then reject the remaining candidates. Keep all correspondence, applications and interview notes on file for three months in the event that your first choice proves to be unsuitable, or a failed candidate decides to take you to an industrial tribunal (see Chapter 7).

Summary

Question   What is the main purpose of a selection interview?
Answer   As recruitment is a two-way process, a selection interview serves a dual purpose. It enables you to see if a candidate matches the employee specification well enough to do the job properly. It allows a candidate to decide if this is the right company and job opportunity for him.

Question   How can this dual purpose be achieved?
Answer   A quiet room must be made available so that you and the candidate can relax and concentrate on each other. Plenty of time should be set aside so that the exchange of information is not rushed. An interview plan – outlining the key topics and questions to be asked – should be drawn up so that all the important areas of mutual interest are covered.

Question   How should an interview be carried out?
Answer   Begin by putting the candidate at ease so he'll talk more freely about himself. Discuss the company and job for a few minutes. Move on to check facts, education, work experience, outside interests, anomalies and ambitions. Use open, closed, limited and hypothetical questions. Avoid leading, multiple and discriminatory ones. Conclude by giving the candidate the chance to ask you any questions. Then, promptly end the interview by standing up, thanking him for coming in and telling him when you'll be in touch.

Question   How can a selection decision be reached?
Answer   Assemble all the information about each candidate and compare it with the employee specification. The candidate who matches it most closely should be chosen.

6　Testing candidates

For many lower grade jobs, in an office or on the shop or factory floor, the recruitment decision will be made after reading application forms, conducting interviews and taking up references. For higher grade jobs, trainee management up to senior positions, where the cost of choosing the wrong person can be especially great, tests are playing an increasingly significant role in the recruitment process. If you are thinking of introducing tests into your company as an aid to decision making, you'll need to know how to set about it. You should be aware of the main types of test that are most widely used – general aptitude, specific aptitude and personality tests. You may want to consider group testing as well.

Introducing tests

The traditional method of assessing a potential new employee (application form/interview/references) can have serious flaws, although a careful, thorough approach should reduce these to a minimum. Application forms may be badly designed and incorrectly screened. Interviews could be poorly located in a noisy, intrusive environment where the candidate feels so edgy that he becomes inhibited. A referee, perhaps anxious to offload a surplus member of his team, may be less candid than you would wish. Furthermore, certain qualities are notoriously difficult to evaluate with any degree of accuracy with such an approach. Intelligence (measured by general aptitude tests), the various skills needed to do the job well (assessed by specific aptitude tests) and personality (judged by personality tests) are hard to gauge from just an application form, where a friend or relative may have assisted and an interview, when the candidate is on his best behaviour.

This then is the key advantage of using tests alongside other such established methods. They should be seen strictly as an aid, not as a replacement – application forms and interviews have far more benefits than drawbacks if used properly. Testing candidates can help to create a more comprehensive picture of them than you might otherwise obtain. With test results measured on a scientific basis (against averages based on the known performances of thousands of other similar people who have sat the test), it should also be more accurate and reliable than when subject to personal interpretation.

Nevertheless, the advantage of objectivity needs to be weighed against the possible disadvantages. Testing is a highly specialized area, and reputable tests take years to be developed, tested and checked for validity and reliability before being used. No manager should devise his own tests unless he is fully trained and sufficiently experienced; nor should he run other, professionally designed tests without first having been through an appropriate training programme which, incidentally, will not necessarily make him capable of running any other test. If a novice compiles and/or administers tests then it will always be a waste of his time and money, invariably producing dubious results and often leading to the wrong choice of candidate. The costs of this – poor performance, absences, re-recruitment – will far outstrip the expense of professional help and advice in the first place.

Bear in mind the financial outlay involved in testing candidates as well. Although this can vary considerably depending on the test publisher and types of test required, a typical training course to enable you successfully to administer, score and interpret a particular test might cost from around £500 (two days) to £1300 (five days) per person. The reference sets, manuals, test sheets, answer booklets, scoring charts and so on that are needed for you to run the test on a dozen candidates or so might cost about £100 or more. (These are very approximate 1991 figures and are exclusive of VAT). Consider the additional expenses involved in travelling to and from courses, absences from work and the actual time taken in running the test on would-be recruits. Weigh the costs against the importance of the job to the company. Only use the test if you cannot obtain the same, equally accurate information in another way (perhaps from a second, more detailed interview).

Should you decide to incorporate tests within your recruitment policy, contact either the British Psychological Society or the Institute of Personnel Management (see Appendix C for a list of the limited number of test suppliers in the country). Alternatively, talk to business associates who may personally recommend one to you. Discuss with them the type of job you want to fill, referring to job analysis notes and the job description, and the person required, as per the employee specification. Talk about the various tests that may be appropriate in the circumstances. Attend the training course, without which tests will not be supplied by a reputable company. Run tests according to the strict guidelines. Always be prepared to go on further refresher courses when necessary and keep up to date with other (better) tests that may be introduced which could help to improve your recruitment methods even more.

General aptitude tests

Before approaching a test supplier, you will find it helpful to know more about the various types of test that may be offered to you. General aptitude tests, also commonly known as general intelligence or mental ability tests, are normally used to assess candidates below graduate level, although some tests are available for graduate and other high ability candidates applying for management and technical posts. With a mixture of words, symbols, numbers and shapes, a candidate is typically expected to fill in a gap (TEA . . . . . BOARD) or complete a sequence (4 . . 9 . . 19 . . 39 . . . . . .?) usually within a set time limit (perhaps 30 to 60 minutes). In some tests, he may be given a number of answers to choose from.

Such tests, similar to the 11 plus or IQ tests with which you'll be familiar – measure and assess the candidate in a number of ways. Those involving words allow you to judge his verbal ability and how well he understands and can deal with verbal concepts. Symbols enable you to evaluate his non-verbal ability to process and differentiate between relevant and irrelevant data. Numerical ability can be gauged from those questions using numbers, showing how well the candidate reasons with figures. Spatial ability, of key significance in design and construction work, may be estimated by the way he

GENERAL ABILITY TESTS
A TEST TAKER'S GUIDE

You have been sent this leaflet to help you prepare for your testing session. It:

* introduces you to the tests themselves;

* gives you an idea of what to expect;

* provides hints on how to prepare yourself;

* answers key questions; but remember that you can still ask questions at the testing session.

Here are the answers to some important questions.

Q   Why am I being asked to take some tests?

A   You may have school or work qualifications, but these tests give extra information which will help employers to select those applicants who are best suited to the job or their training programme.

Tests also help you to explore your abilities; this should assist you in choosing a suitable area of work.

People who are successful in the job have usually done well in the tests, so both employers and applicants get what they want.

Q   How do they work?

A   Employers decide which skills and abilities are needed in the job. Tests are then selected to measure some of these.

There is a practice period in the testing session to make sure everyone understands how to do the test(s).

The tests are carefully timed, so you may not finish; but you should work as fast as you can and follow the instructions given.

Your answers are then scored and this information is used to help decide whether you will be suitable for the job.

Q   Will I be asked to do anything else?

A   Usually you will be asked to fill in an application form and this information is also very important.

You may also be interviewed. Employers use information from many sources to help them make the best decision.

THE TEST SESSION

When you come to the session you will be asked to do the tests ticked below. The time shown beside each test is the time you will be allowed once you have been given the introductory examples and practice test. Remember you will be given a break between the tests.

_____ **Verbal**	15 minutes
_____ **Numerical**	20 minutes
_____ **Non-Verbal**	20 minutes
_____ **Spatial**	20 minutes

Look at the examples given for each of the tests you will be taking. None of these examples will be in the real tests.

Check that you understand the questions and correct answers. Remember that if you do not understand there will be time to ask before the test begins.

Figure 6.1   GAT Test Taker's Guide

THE ANSWER SHEET

You will be given a separate answer sheet for each test. The one given below is from the Verbal Test and is marked with the correct answers for the examples given. The Numerical and Non-Verbal answer sheets are very similar.

```
1   A ◼ C D E F      13  A B C D E F      25  A B C D E F
2   ◼ B C D E F      14  A B C D E F      26  A B C D E F
3   A B C D E F      15  A B C D E F      27  A B C D E F
4   A B C D E F      16  A B C D E F      28  A B C D E F
5   A B C D E F      17  A B C D E F      29  A B C D E F
6   A B C D E F      18  A B C D E F      30  A B C D E F
```

Below is a section from the Spatial answer sheet. The correct answers to Examples 1 to 4 are marked.

```
1   ◼ N     17  Y N     33  Y N     49  Y N     65  Y N
2   ◼ N     18  Y N     34  Y N     50  Y N     66  Y N
3   Y ◼     19  Y N     35  Y N     51  Y N     67  Y N
4   ◼ N     20  Y N     36  Y N     52  Y N     68  Y N
5   Y N     21  Y N     37  Y N     53  Y N     69  Y N
6   Y N     22  Y N     38  Y N     54  Y N     70  Y N
7   Y N     23  Y N     39  Y N     55  Y N     71  Y N
8   Y N     24  Y N     40  Y N     56  Y N     72  Y N
```

VERBAL

This test is about relationships between pairs of words. In each question you are given one pair of words and you have to find out how they are related. Then you have to choose a word, from the six given, which would complete another pair of words. The missing word is shown by a question mark. The second pair must be related to each other in the same way as the pair you have been given.

In the two examples below the correct answers are highlighted: '**clothes**' is the answer to Example 1, and '**line**' is the answer to Example 2.

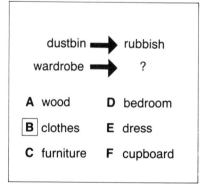

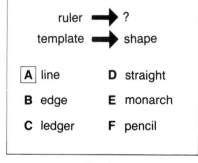

Example 1   Example 2

Figure 6.1   *continued*

NON-VERBAL

In this test you have to work out relationships between shapes. There are two basic types of question. In the first, as Example 1, you are given two large figures inside an oval. You have to decide how they are alike, which may be in one way or several ways. Only one figure at the bottom also has all these qualities. In this case there is a small shape followed by a dotted line, then two solid lines. Only figure **A** fits this description. The correct answer has been highlighted.

In the other questions, such as Examples 2 and 3, there is a grid which contains an arrangement of shapes with one missing section. This is marked by the question mark. You have to decide how the shapes are related to each other and decide which of the six possibilities is the missing one.

In Example 2, the three figures in the centre of each big triangle are repeated in the outer triangles next to them. Also, each repeated figure has either a circle or a triangle around it. Here, the answer is '**F**'.

In Example 3, a different grid is used. The answer, which is '**A**', can be found by looking at the pattern of shapes in the inside and outside triangles.

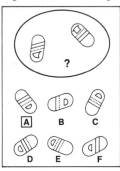

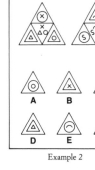

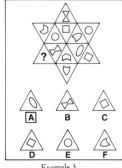

| Example 1 | Example 2 | Example 3 |

NUMERICAL

In this test you have to work out the relationship between numbers. All questions have an arrangement of numbers in a grid with one or two numbers missing. The missing numbers are shown by question marks. You have to find how the numbers are related to each other and so decide which of the six possibilities is the missing one.

If you look at the first example below, the numbers in the 'chain' on the left-hand side go in sequence by 'doubling up'. Thus, twice 3 is 6; twice 6 is 12; and twice 12 is 24. Therefore the missing answer is **24** or '**C**'. The correct answer has been highlighted.

Sometimes you have two numbers missing and you will have to find the answer which has them both. In Example 2 you have to look across the rows and down the columns rather like a crossword. Going across the rows, the numbers increase by the same amount; going down the rows they double each time. You must find the two numbers that fit both of these rules. The missing numbers are **14** and **20**, which is answer '**A**'.

In Example 3, you again must find the two missing numbers. Here, the bottom number on the left is always 21 more than the top number, and the one on the right is always 10 more than the top numbers. Thus, the correct answer is '**A**'.

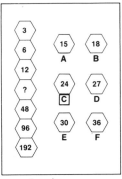

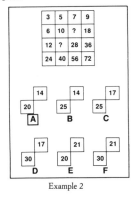

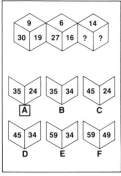

| Example 1 | Example 2 | Example 3 |

Figure 6.1 *continued*

SPATIAL

In this test you have to imagine what a flat pattern would look like if it were cut out and folded into a solid object. The patterns have to be folded along the black lines so that the markings are on the outside of the solid object.

You have to decide if each of the solid objects shown below the flat pattern could be made from it when folded. Answer 'no' if an object definitely **could not** be made and 'yes' if it definitely **could** be made. If you cannot be sure without seeing the hidden side, answer 'yes'.

In Example 1, if the pattern were folded it would form a long shape with one black side and the dot in the middle on one of the ends. Question 1 clearly could be this shape with the black side and dot in the correct places. Similarly, the answer to question 2 is 'yes' since there is one black side and you can only see one of the ends; the other one could have the dot on it. However, the answer to question 3 is clearly 'no' since the long side on the top left should be black. Question 4 is 'yes' because the black side is hidden under the shape. The correct answers are under the questions.

In Example 2 the answers to questions 5, 6 and 7 are 'yes', while the answer to 8 is 'no'.

Example 1

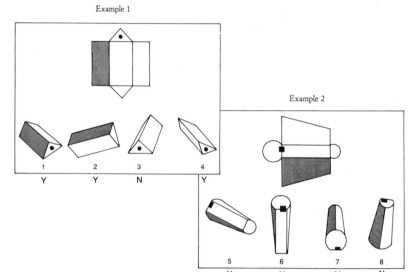

Example 2

Q   How can I prepare myself for the test?

*   Prepare yourself by having a good night's sleep and arriving well in time.

*   If you normally wear glasses or a hearing aid remember to bring them with you.

*   Read this leaflet carefully and make sure you understand what to expect from the tests you will be doing.

Q   How do I do my best in the tests?

*   Don't be afraid to ask a question if there is something not clear to you.

*   Listen carefully and follow the instructions given as well as you can.

*   Remember that most tests are timed, so work quickly and accurately without wasting time on those questions you do not understand.

*   If it is a long time since you did an exam or test, do not worry! Test results, if used correctly, should give a fair assessment regardless of your age, race, sex or background.

Figure 6.1   *concluded*

handles questions involving shapes. Typically, a candidate may have to imagine how a flat pattern would look as a three-dimensional object.

Tests of verbal, non-verbal, numerical and spatial ability, often mixed together in one general test, will not guarantee that a successful candidate (as compared to the 'average') will do a job well. Nevertheless, they will show that he has the ability to reason in a variety of ways, can think quickly and is capable of learning new information. These must surely be important qualities in any job.

ASE – a division of NFER-NELSON, Britain's largest publisher of tests – has devised a series of *General Ability Tests (GAT)* which provide good examples of this type of test. It consists of four short tests which may be used on their own to assess a particular general ability (verbal, non-verbal, numerical, spatial) or together to produce a more complete picture of the candidate.

Special test taker's guides can be sent to candidates beforehand so that they may become familiar with the type of questions they will face. Worked examples of the four tests are given and you can indicate those which you intend to use. The verbal test lasts for 15 minutes, with the non-verbal, numerical and spatial running for 20 minutes each. See Figure 6.1, Copyright © 1988. Reproduced with permission of ASE, a division of the NFER-NELSON Publishing Company Limited.

Specific aptitude tests

In addition to finding out about a candidate's general intelligence, you may also want to know whether he has any specific talents such as a flair for learning languages quickly (have you listed any essential or desirable talents on the employee specification?) These tests, otherwise called special ability tests, can be used to measure the innate skills which are needed or need to be developed to do the job properly.

A bewildering array of professionally devised tests is available to assess almost every ability imaginable including mechanical reasoning, manual dexterity and computer programming, word processing and clerical abilities. Also on offer are tests to measure specific forms of verbal, numerical and spatial reasoning. Should you be seriously considering using them, don't forget to ask yourself whether such tests are absolutely necessary (How important is the job?). You may perhaps be able to make an appropriate assessment in another way, possibly obtaining references as to past performances which could accurately reflect likely future performance.

As examples of specific aptitude tests, ASE market *Modern Occupational Skills Tests (MOST)* which can help you to choose a candidate with those administrative skills and aptitudes that may be important attributes for secretarial and clerical staff, junior management and supervisory positions. Having identified the essential tasks of the job (with the aid of MOST's Task Inventory and your job description), you select the four most appropriate tests from the nine that are available.

These nine tests cover separate key skills and are grouped at three levels, according to difficulty. At the first level, there are Verbal Checking, Numerical Checking and Filing tests. Verbal Checking measures a candidate's speed and accuracy at cross-referencing information. Over a period of eight minutes, he has to check various handwritten and printed items including rental agreements, lists of names and minutes of meetings. Numerical Checking is similar, where a candidate is expected to check printed and handwritten numerical items such as prices, dates and computer codes. Again, eight minutes is available. The Filing test evaluates a candidate's ability to file, categorize and code using increasingly complicated systems. Up to twelve minutes can be taken for this particular test.

Numerical Awareness, Spelling and Grammar and Word Meanings tests are gathered together at the second level, with eight, eight and twelve minutes respectively set aside for each one.

Numerical Awareness measures a candidate's arithmetical ability. He is expected to spot and amend numerical errors in totals, receipts and timetables. Spelling and Grammar assesses spelling and grammatical ability which is so important for those employees who are expected to draft, correct or check reports, memoranda and correspondence. Word Meanings evaluates a candidate's range and depth of vocabulary. Errors in notices, minutes and letters have to be seen and corrected.

At the third – and most difficult – level are tests of Numerical Estimation, Technical Checking and Decision Making. Accordingly, 12, 12 and 15 minutes are allowed for each test. Numerical Estimation measures a candidate's potential for estimating quickly and accurately. It is particularly relevant when selecting employees who will be working in marketing, finance and data processing. Technical Checking assesses the ability to cross-check information presented in a variety of formats such as graphs and display screens. Decision Making evaluates a candidate's ability to assess, prioritize and categorize

MODERN OCCUPATIONAL SKILLS TESTS
VERBAL CHECKING
A TEST TAKER'S GUIDE

Part of our organization's selection system involves the use of tests. The reason for using tests is simply to collect as much information as possible about each person to help us make a more informed and fairer decision.

This leaflet has been sent to you to help you prepare for your testing session. It:

★ introduces you to each test;
★ gives you an idea of what to expect;
★ provides hints on how best to prepare yourself;
★ answers key questions (but remember you can still ask questions at the testing session)

Here are the answers to some important questions:

Q. Why am I being asked to take some tests?
A. You may have various qualifications and experience, but these tests give extra information to employers.

Q. How do they work?
A. Employers decide which skills and abilities are needed in the job. Tests are then selected to measure some of these. There is a practice period in each test to make sure everybody understands how to do the test(s). The tests are carefully timed, so you might not finish; however work as fast as you can and follow the instructions given. Your answers are then scored and will influence our final decision. People are not selected on test results alone.

THE TEST SESSION

When you come to the test session you will be asked to do ___ tests. Remember if there is more than one test you will be given a break between each test.

Look at the example overleaf. It is for the VERBAL CHECKING test and will last eight minutes. None of the examples will be in the real tests. Check you understand the questions and answers. If you do not understand there will be time to ask before the test begins.

In this test you have to find errors in various kinds of documents. In each question, the material in the **shaded answer box** has some errors. Put a ring around each of the errors you find, which may include missing words, when you check the answer box against the other version. Look at the following example.

Figure 6.2   MOST Test Taker's Guides

Verbal Checking

Below is a handwritten list of references for a journal article. Check the typed list in the answer box and ring any errors.

References

Buxted, J. P. (1984) Finding your feet: New approaches to ambulatory therapy. American Journal of Ambulatory Medicine, 4, 6, 31–42.

Parandreus A. A. and Lee Wu C. (1985) Pain and training. British Journal of Sport Psychology, 2, 2, 256–282.

Williams B. (1981) Metacarpal distress: The perils of overtraining. Sports medicine, 4, 1, 92–98.

Answer box

References

Buxted J. (R.) (1984) Finding your feet: New approaches to ambulatory therapy. **American Journal of** (Ambulance) Medicine, 4,6,31-42.

(Papandreus) A. A. and Lee Wu C. (1985) Pain and training. British Journal of Sport Psychology, 2,2,256-282.

Williams B. (1981) (Metatarsal) distress: The perils of overtraining. (Sporting) medicine, 4,1,92-98.

If you make a mistake, cross it out like this (Smith ⦸) , then ring the correct answer.

Figure 6.2 *continued*

MODERN OCCUPATIONAL SKILLS TESTS
NUMERICAL CHECKING
A TEST TAKER'S GUIDE

Part of our organization's selection system involves the use of tests. The reason for using tests is simply to collect as much information as possible about each person to help us make a more informed and fairer decision.

This leaflet has been sent to you to help you prepare for your testing session. It:

★ introduces you to each test;
★ gives you an idea of what to expect;
★ provides hints on how best to prepare yourself;
★ answers key questions (but remember you can still ask questions at the testing session)

Here are the answers to some important questions:

Q. Why am I being asked to take some tests?
A. You may have various qualifications and experience, but these tests give extra information to employers.

Q. How do they work?
A. Employers decide which skills and abilities are needed in the job. Tests are then selected to measure some of these. There is a practice period in each test to make sure everybody understands how to do the test(s). The tests are carefully timed, so you might not finish; however work as fast as you can and follow the instructions given. Your answers are then scored and will influence our final decision. People are not selected on test results alone.

THE TEST SESSION

When you come to the test session you will be asked to do ___ tests. Remember if there is more than one test you will be given a break between each test.

Look at the example overleaf. It is for the NUMERICAL CHECKING test and will last eight minutes. None of the examples will be in the real tests. Check you understand the questions and answers. If you do not understand there will be time to ask before the test begins.

In this test you have to find errors in various tables of numbers. In each question the material in the **shaded answer box** has some errors. Put a circle around each of the errors you find when you check the answer box against the other version. Look at the following example.

Figure 6.2   *continued*

Numerical Checking

Errors have crept into a computer file. Fortunately you have a back-up file which is correct. Ring the errors in the file in the answer box.

Index	Sex	Age	Status		Index	Sex	Age	Status
					Answer box			
00412	1	36	15/24		00412	1	36	15/24
00413	2	23	15/30		00413	2	(25)	15/30
00541	1	49	12/08		(00441)	1	49	12/08
00589	1	18	12/08		00589	1	18	12(09)
00724	2	20	12/08		00724	2	20	12/08
00893	1	57	15/24		00893	1	57	15/24
00895	2	52	08/30		00895	(1)	52	08/30
01002	2	34	15/30		(00102)	2	34	15(24)
00117	2	29	08/24		00117	2	29	08/24
01126	1	27	08/24		01126	1	27	08/24

If you make a mistake, cross it out like this and ring the correct answer.

Figure 6.2   *continued*

MODERN OCCUPATIONAL SKILLS TESTS
FILING
A TEST TAKER'S GUIDE

Part of our organization's selection system involves the use of tests. The reason for using tests is simply to collect as much information as possible about each person to help us make a more informed and fairer decision.

This leaflet has been sent to you to help you prepare for your testing session. It:

★ introduces you to each test;
★ gives you an idea of what to expect;
★ provides hints on how best to prepare yourself;
★ answers key questions (but remember you can still ask questions at the testing session)

Here are the answers to some important questions:

Q. Why am I being asked to take some tests?
A. You may have various qualifications and experience, but these tests give extra information to employers.

Q. How do they work?
A. Employers decide which skills and abilities are needed in the job. Tests are then selected to measure some of these. There is a practice period in each test to make sure everybody understands how to do the test(s). The tests are carefully timed, so you might not finish; however work as fast as you can and follow the instructions given. Your answers are then scored and will influence our final decision. People are not selected on test results alone.

THE TEST SESSION

When you come to the test session you will be asked to do ___ tests. Remember if there is more than one test you will be given a break between each test.

Look at the example overleaf. It is for the FILING test and will last 12 minutes. None of the examples will be in the real tests. Check you understand the questions and answers. If you do not understand there will be time to ask before the test begins.

In this test, you have to put new records in the right place in a filing system. In each question, there is a file with numbered records and a list of new records with no record numbers. Decide where each record should go and write, in the answer boxes, the numbers of the two records between which it should be placed. Look at the following example.

Figure 6.2   *continued*

Filing

Below is the personnel file of a small department of a larger company. It is organized firstly by the year of joining the company and then alphabetically by name.

Record No.	Name	Date joined company	Job Title	Date of birth	Date left company
1	Atkins J. P.	4/12/84	Accounts Clerk	5/4/62	15/9/86
2	Davies E.	15/7/84	Secretary	23/8/64	
3	Gadsdon S. B.	21/3/84	Office Manager	18/7/42	20/4/87
4	Hefferen J. C.	19/11/84	Accounts Clerk	9/12/52	1/3/87
5	Eraclens H. P.	27/1/85	Revenue Clerk	21/11/63	10/6/86
6	Pascall N. A.	2/9/85	Revenue Clerk	30/4/40	
7	Price S. M.	15/6/85	Revenue Clerk	2/9/54	12/5/88
8	Maydon A. P.	16/6/86	Revenue Clerk	15/7/60	
9	Prime A. G.	29/9/86	Accounts Clerk	19/6/61	12/10/87
10	Davies J.	14/10/87	Accounts Clerk	4/10/59	
11	Sabel D.	21/4/87	Office Manager	11/1/60	
12	Speck G. C.	3/3/87	Accounts Clerk	22/1/47	
13	Walgama C. R.	19/5/88	Revenue Clerk	9/4/69	

Between which two records would the following members of staff have been placed?

Answer box

1. George Ferris, who was recruited in January 1985, aged 32, to a general clerical position. | 5 and 6 |
2. Eloise Mary Pink, born 5/9/61, who joined as an accounts clerk on 3rd September 1985 and left on 6th January 1988. | 6 and 7 |
3. Patricia Challis, a revenue clerk, who joined on 3/6/86 and is still with the company. | 7 and 8 |

If you make a mistake, cross it out like this ⊠ and ⟨ 7 ⟩ , or ⟨ 6 ⟩ and ⊠ , or ⊠ and ⊠ , then write in the correct answer alongside.

Figure 6.2 *continued*

MODERN OCCUPATIONAL SKILLS TESTS
NUMERICAL AWARENESS
A TEST TAKER'S GUIDE

Part of our organization's selection system involves the use of tests. The reason for using tests is simply to collect as much information as possible about each person to help us make a more informed and fairer decision.

This leaflet has been sent to you to help you prepare for your testing session. It:

★ introduces you to each test;
★ gives you an idea of what to expect;
★ provides hints on how best to prepare yourself;
★ answers key questions (but remember you can still ask questions at the testing session)

Here are the answers to some important questions:

Q. Why am I being asked to take some tests?
A. You may have various qualifications and experience, but these tests give extra information to employers.

Q. How do they work?
A. Employers decide which skills and abilities are needed in the job. Tests are then selected to measure some of these. There is a practice period in each test to make sure everybody understands how to do the test(s). The tests are carefully timed, so you might not finish; however work as fast as you can and follow the instructions given. Your answers are then scored and will influence our final decision. People are not selected on test results alone.

THE TEST SESSION

When you come to the test session you will be asked to do ___ tests. Remember if there is more than one test you will be given a break between each test.

Look at the example overleaf. It is for the NUMERICAL AWARENESS test and will last eight minutes. None of the examples will be in the real tests. Check you understand the questions and answers. If you do not understand there will be time to ask before the test begins.

Figure 6.2   *continued*

In this test you have to find and correct errors in calculations. Each question consists of a set of calculations and a final total. The information on which the calculations are based is always correct. However **one** calculation in each question has been done incorrectly. **The error is always found in the totals column.** Your task is to score out all incorrect amounts and to write the correct amounts in the answer boxes. Note, however, that the incorrect calculations will affect the final total in every question and may affect the final sub-totals. These totals must also be corrected. Look at the example below.

Numerical Awareness

La Fontanella Restaurant		Table 6	Total	Answer box
2	Steak au poivre	@ £6.50	£13.00	
2	Sole Veronique	@ £6.00	£12.00	
3	Paté â la maison	@ £1.50	£4.50	
1	Avocado Vinaigrette	@ £1.50	£1.50	
4	Creme Caramel	@ £1.25	£6.00	5.00
1	Chateau Le Lion	@ £7.50	£7.50	
1	Barolo	@ £9.50	£9.50	
4	Coffee	@ £1.00	£4.00	
			£58.00	57.00
		Service Charge @ 10%	£5.80	5.70
		Total	£63.80	62.70

Four Creme Caramels at £1.25 comes to £5.00 and not £6.00. The sub-total should, therefore, be £57.00 and not £58.00, the service charge should equal £5.70 and the Total Charge £62.70.

If you make a mistake, cross it out like this |__2.80__| then write the correct answer alongside.

Figure 6.2 *continued*

MODERN OCCUPATIONAL SKILLS TESTS
SPELLING AND GRAMMAR
A TEST TAKER'S GUIDE

Part of our organization's selection system involves the use of tests. The reason for using tests is simply to collect as much information as possible about each person to help us make a more informed and fairer decision.

This leaflet has been sent to you to help you prepare for your testing session. It:

★ introduces you to each test;
★ gives you an idea of what to expect;
★ provides hints on how best to prepare yourself;
★ answers key questions (but remember you can still ask questions at the testing session)

Here are the answers to some important questions:

Q. Why am I being asked to take some tests?
A. You may have various qualifications and experience, but these tests give extra information to employers.

Q. How do they work?
A. Employers decide which skills and abilities are needed in the job. Tests are then selected to measure some of these. There is a practice period in each test to make sure everybody understands how to do the test(s). The tests are carefully timed, so you might not finish; however work as fast as you can and follow the instructions given. Your answers are then scored and will influence our final decision. People are not selected on test results alone.

THE TEST SESSION

When you come to the test session you will be asked to do __ tests. Remember if there is more than one test you will be given a break between each test.

Look at the example overleaf. It is for the SPELLING AND GRAMMAR test and will last eight minutes. None of the examples will be in the real tests. Check you understand the questions and answers. If you do not understand there will be time to ask before the test begins.

In this test you have to find errors of spelling and grammar. Each question consists of a document which contains several of each kind of error. Draw a ring around each of the errors you find. Look at the following example.

Figure 6.2 *continued*

Spelling and Grammar

Dear Sir,

Please find enclosed an ⟨estemate⟩ for carrying out the repairs to your property ⟨what⟩ we discussed on Monday. You will see that I think it is advisable ⟨of us⟩ to apply ⟨stabalising⟩ fluid in the preparation of the stucco and that it will be necessary to cut out the ⟨roted⟩ section of the defective plinth. I cannot find any ⟨quory⟩ iles which will fit your kitchen so I will have to cut ⟨it⟩ If you want more information yo⟨u⟩ contact me at the above number.

Yours sincerely,

Explanation of Errors

1. Estimate with an "i" and not an "e".
2. "What" is ungrammatical. It could be omitted or replaced by "that" or "which".
3. "of us" is also ungrammatical. It would be omitted or replaced by "for us".
4. "stabilising" should be spelt "bil" and not bal".
5. "rotted" should be spelt with two t's.
6. "quarry" is spelt with an "a" and not an "o" and has two "r"s.
7. "it" is ungrammatical and should be replaced by "them".
8. The word "can" should be inserted between "you" and "contact".

If you make a mistake, cross it out like this ⟨houses⟩, then ring the correct word or words.

Figure 6.2   *continued*

MODERN OCCUPATIONAL SKILLS TESTS
WORD MEANINGS
A TEST TAKER'S GUIDE

Part of our organization's selection system involves the use of tests. The reason for using tests is simply to collect as much information as possible about each person to help us make a more informed and fairer decision.

This leaflet has been sent to you to help you prepare for your testing session. It:

★ introduces you to each test;
★ gives you an idea of what to expect;
★ provides hints on how best to prepare yourself;
★ answers key questions (but remember you can still ask questions at the testing session)

Here are the answers to some important questions:

Q. Why am I being asked to take some tests?
A. You may have various qualifications and experience, but these tests give extra information to employers.

Q. How do they work?
A. Employers decide which skills and abilities are needed in the job. Tests are then selected to measure some of these. There is a practice period in each test to make sure everybody understands how to do the test(s). The tests are carefully timed, so you might not finish; however work as fast as you can and follow the instructions given. Your answers are then scored and will influence our final decision. People are not selected on test results alone.

THE TEST SESSION

When you come to the test session you will be asked to do __ tests. Remember if there is more than one test you will be given a break between each test.

Look at the example overleaf. It is for the WORD MEANINGS test and will last 12 minutes. None of the examples will be in the real tests. Check you understand the questions and answers. If you do not understand there will be time to ask before the test begins.

In this test you have to find words which have been used incorrectly and replace them with suitable words. Each question consists of a document which contains several incorrectly used words. When you find an incorrect word in a line choose a replacement from the list of words provided and write its identifying letter in the answer box beside that line. Look at the following example.

Figure 6.2   *continued*

Word Meanings

Answer box
F
C
B
K

All essence repairs required to be carried out as a condition of the offer of a mortgage should be done to a satisfactory standard. The Building Society must be informed of the repetition of the repairs and sent copies of the contractors receipted accounts if appointed. A re-inspection will only be carried out if you digest it even when this is a condition of the offer.

A	accountable	E	consideration	I	interests
B	appropriate	F	essential	J	permission
C	completion	G	final	K	request
D	connection	H	invoices	L	repayment

If you make a mistake cross it out like this ̶A̶----B̶-- then write the correct answer alongside.

Figure 6.2 *continued*

MODERN OCCUPATIONAL SKILLS TESTS
NUMERICAL ESTIMATION
A TEST TAKER'S GUIDE

Part of our organization's selection system involves the use of tests. The reason for using tests is simply to collect as much information as possible about each person to help us make a more informed and fairer decision.

This leaflet has been sent to you to help you prepare for your testing session. It:

★ introduces you to each test;
★ gives you an idea of what to expect;
★ provides hints on how best to prepare yourself;
★ answers key questions (but remember you can still ask questions at the testing session)

Here are the answers to some important questions:

Q. Why am I being asked to take some tests?
A. You may have various qualifications and experience, but these tests give extra information to employers.

Q. How do they work?
A. Employers decide which skills and abilities are needed in the job. Tests are then selected to measure some of these. There is a practice period in each test to make sure everybody understands how to do the test(s). The tests are carefully timed, so you might not finish; however work as fast as you can and follow the instructions given. Your answers are then scored and will influence our final decision. People are not selected on test results alone.

THE TEST SESSION

When you come to the test session you will be asked to do ___ tests. Remember if there is more than one test you will be given a break between each test.

Look at the example overleaf. It is for the NUMERICAL ESTIMATION test and will last 12 minutes. None of the examples will be in the real tests. Check you understand the questions and answers. If you do not understand there will be time to ask before the test begins.

In this test you have to give approximate answers to complex calculations. Each question consists of a calculation which is too difficult to do in your head, and there is not enough time to work it out exactly on paper. Instead, on each page you are given a list of numbers with boxes alongside them. Your task is to mark **two adjacent boxes** with solid horizontal lines, like this ⊟ indicating the two numbers which are closest to the real answer.

Figure 6.2   *continued*

Look at the example below.

Numerical Estimation

A lorry averages 10.18 miles to the gallon. During the next five days it is going to be used on four journeys of 226 miles, 147 miles, 402 miles and 228 miles. How many gallons of fuel will it use on these journeys?

50 gallons	☐
70 gallons	☐
90 gallons	▬
110 gallons	▬
130 gallons	☐
150 gallons	☐
170 gallons	☐

The four journeys add up to slightly more than 1000 miles. The lorry does only slightly more than 10 miles to the gallon. It will therefore use close to 100 gallons of fuel on the journeys, and the 90 gallons and 110 gallons boxes should be marked to show the two values nearest to the actual value.

If you make a mistake cross it out like this   **then mark the correct box(es).**

Figure 6.2   *continued*

MODERN OCCUPATIONAL SKILLS TESTS
TECHNICAL CHECKING
A TEST TAKER'S GUIDE

Part of our organization's selection system involves the use of tests. The reason for using tests is simply to collect as much information as possible about each person to help us make a more informed and fairer decision.

This leaflet has been sent to you to help you prepare for your testing session. It:

* ★ introduces you to each test;
* ★ gives you an idea of what to expect;
* ★ provides hints on how best to prepare yourself;
* ★ answers key questions (but remember you can still ask questions at the testing session)

Here are the answers to some important questions:

Q. Why am I being asked to take some tests?
A. You may have various qualifications and experience, but these tests give extra information to employers.

Q. How do they work?
A. Employers decide which skills and abilities are needed in the job. Tests are then selected to measure some of these. There is a practice period in each test to make sure everybody understands how to do the test(s). The tests are carefully timed, so you might not finish; however work as fast as you can and follow the instructions given. Your answers are then scored and will influence our final decision. People are not selected on test results alone.

THE TEST SESSION

When you come to the test session you will be asked to do ___ tests. Remember if there is more than one test you will be given a break between each test.

Look at the example overleaf. It is for the TECHNICAL CHECKING test and will last 12 minutes. None of the examples will be in the real tests. Check you understand the questions and answers. If you do not understand there will be time to ask before the test begins.

In this test you have to find errors in various kinds of documents. In each question the same material is shown in two different forms. There are some errors in the shaded answer box. Put a circle around each of the errors you find when you check the answer box against the other version. Look at the following example.

Figure 6.2 *continued*

Technical Checking

Below is a map of a tourist circuit. Check the instructions for the journey round the circuit and ring any errors.

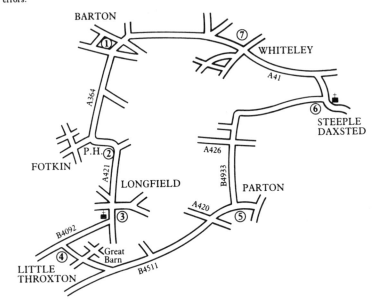

Instructions

1. Leave the town of Barton on the A364. Continue to the ouskirts of the village of (Firkin).
2. Turn left at the Fox and Hound public house and follow the A421 to Longfield.
3. Turn right at Longfield church onto the (B4492).
4. Turn left from the B4092 to the village of Little Throxton. Turn (right) at the Great Barn onto the B4511.
5. Cross over the A420 to the village of Parton and turn left just before the church onto the B4933.
6. In the village of (Steep) Daxsted, turn left at the church onto the A41.
7. Stay on the A41 through the village of Whiteley back to Barton.

If you make a mistake, cross it out like this £ | (40) 94 | then ring the correct answer.

Figure 6.2 *continued*

MODERN OCCUPATIONAL SKILLS TESTS
DECISION MAKING
A TEST TAKER'S GUIDE

Part of our organization's selection system involves the use of tests. The reason for using tests is simply to collect as much information as possible about each person to help us make a more informed and fairer decision.

This leaflet has been sent to you to help you prepare for your testing session. It:

* introduces you to each test;
* gives you an idea of what to expect;
* provides hints on how best to prepare yourself;
* answers key questions (but remember you can still ask questions at the testing session)

Here are the answers to some important questions:

Q. Why am I being asked to take some tests?
A. You may have various qualifications and experience, but these tests give extra information to employers.

Q. How do they work?
A. Employers decide which skills and abilities are needed in the job. Tests are then selected to measure some of these. There is a practice period in each test to make sure everybody understands how to do the test(s). The tests are carefully timed, so you might not finish; however work as fast as you can and follow the instructions given. Your answers are then scored and will influence our final decision. People are not selected on test results alone.

THE TEST SESSION

When you come to the test session you will be asked to do ___ tests. Remember if there is more than one test you will be given a break between each test.

Look at the example overleaf. It is for the DECISION MAKING test and will last 15 minutes. None of the examples will be in the real tests. Check you understand the questions and answers. If you do not understand there will be time to ask before the test begins.

In this test you have to answer enquiries by deciding which options meet an enquirer's needs. Each question has a number of enquiries to answer and a set of rules which are needed to answer the questions. These rules will be found in boxes below the questions. The questions are answered by selecting **one, or more than one,** of the options provided. Find **all** the options which fit the rules and mark the appropriate answer boxes with **solid horizontal lines.** Look at the following example.

Figure 6.2   *continued*

Decision Making

A company gives discounts on its products at one of four rates. The rules for deciding whether and how large a discount can be given are shown below. What discount would you give each of the following three customers:

1. A customer who is going to pay cash for goods worth £1500.

No discount
5% discount
10% discount
15% discount
20% discount

2. A customer who wants to pay for £400 worth of goods over a nine month period

No discount
5% discount
10% discount
15% discount
20% discount

3. A customer who wants to buy £800 worth of goods and pay for them over four months.

No discount
5% discount
10% discount
15% discount
20% discount

Rules

1. Give a 5% discount if the value of the goods sold is greater then £500 but less than £1000.
2. Give a 10% discount if the value of goods sold is greater than £1000.
3. Give a 5% discount if the customer wants credit but will pay within 6 months.
4. Give a 10% discount if the customer does not want credit and will pay immediately.
5. Add together any applicable discounts.

If you make a mistake, cross it out like this then mark the correct box.

Figure 6.2 *concluded*

quickly. It is most appropriate for use on potential administrators and managers.

See Figure 6.2, Copyright © 1989. Reproduced with permission of ASE, a division of the NFER-NELSON Publishing Company Limited.

Personality tests

Personality tests are probably the most widely used selection tests because all employers want to be certain that a candidate will fit in and get on well with other employees. No matter how bright and gifted a new recruit may be, it can become relatively unimportant if he is constantly at loggerheads with his colleagues and the work rate and performance of the entire department are badly disrupted. Personality tests could thus be of some assistance if you cannot accurately assess candidates' personalities in any other way.

Such tests typically comprise a series of questions (Do you enjoy working to a deadline? Do you like delegating duties to other people?) to which a candidate must reply 'yes' or 'no'. Sometimes, statements will be made (I set schedules for myself. I lose my temper) and he has to circle one of a number of answers (rarely, sometimes, often). Also, comments may be given (The job must always come first. A person's private life should never interfere with his professional life) and a candidate has to state an opinion about it (strongly agree, agree, neutral, disagree, strongly disagree). His answers are then used to draw up a profile of his personality so you can decide if he is a suitable person for the job.

One of the most popular personality tests on the market today is the *Sixteen Personality Factor Questionnaire (16PF)* available from ASE. It is widely used in the selection of graduate, managerial, professional and technical staff. Developed after analysing thousands of responses, it measures each candidate's personality against 16 scales which reflect both behaviour and likely job performance. Untimed, the full version, containing nearly 400 questions, should last around 40 minutes with the short version, comprising approximately 200 questions, running around 25 minutes. See Figure 6.3, Copyright © 1949, 1956, 1962, 1967, 1978. Reproduced with permission of ASE, a division of the NFER-NELSON Publishing Company Limited.

Group tests

Having assessed candidates individually, by reading applications and running interviews and tests, you may wish to bring them together as a group to see how they behave and interact with each other. This can be a valid and extremely important testing method especially where the successful candidate is expected to lead or work as part of a team.

Group testing can be carried out in a variety of ways, according to circumstances. Candidates may be seated, perhaps around a circular table so that no one person is put in a more dominating position, and asked to discuss a subject among themselves. This could be of general interest (Should smoking be forbidden in public places? Should drunken drivers automatically be banned for life?) or might be job-related (Should animals be used for research purposes? for candidates wishing to join a pharmaceutical company or Should the police carry firearms? for candidates wanting to join the police force). Whatever it is, it must obviously be pitched at the right level for the group, so that a lively discussion will follow, and for the individuals concerned, so that they can all contribute equally.

Sometimes, candidates will be given a problem to solve as a team. This should be strictly relevant to the job and should not be solvable unless all of the candidates contribute their various skills and experiences. In the Armed Forces, a typical exercise would involve the candidates taking one of their team with a broken leg and all their equipment across an imaginary river without falling in or breaking any other legs. In business, it might involve data being supplied to the group (perhaps in advance) about a particular market opportunity. They must then discuss and decide which product should be launched, which consumer group should be targeted and so on. Sometimes, a leader will be appointed (with the role possibly changing hands regularly throughout the test). On other occasions, the group will be left on its own to see who the natural leaders are.

Regardless of the approach, group tests will be timed and carefully monitored by assessors sitting unobtrusively nearby. Everything that is said and done by the candidates will be noted down, or even recorded on video if all agree, for subsequent discussion. Ideally, at least two assessors will be allocated to each candidate to help to ensure that fair assessments and decisions are made, free from individual prejudice and bias.

THE SIXTEEN PERSONALITY FACTOR
QUESTIONNAIRE
FORM A

WHAT TO DO: Inside this booklet are some questions to see what attitudes and interests you have. There are no "right" and "wrong" answers because everyone has the right to their own views. To be able to get the best advice from your results, you should want to answer them exactly and truly.

Write your name and all other information asked for on the top line of the Answer Sheet.

First you should answer the four sample questions below so that you can see whether you need to ask anything before starting. Although you are to read the questions in this booklet, you must record your answers on the answer sheet (next to the same number as in the booklet).

There are three possible answers to each question. Read the following examples and mark your answers at the top of your answer sheet where it says "Examples." Fill in the left-hand box if your answer choice is the "a" answer, in the middle box if your answer choice is the "b" answer, and in the right-hand box if you choose the "c" answer.

EXAMPLES:

1.   I like to watch team games.

    a. yes,   b. occasionally,   c. no.

2.   I prefer people who:

    a. are reserved,
    b. (are) in between,
    c. make friends quickly.

3.   Money cannot bring happiness.

    a. yes (true)   b. in between,   c. no (false).

4.   Adult is to child as cat is to:

    a. kitten,   b. dog,   c. boy.

In the last example there *is* a right answer–kitten. But there are very few such reasoning items.

Ask *now* if anything is not clear. The examiner will tell you in a moment to turn the page and start.

When you answer, keep these four points in mind:

1.   You are asked not to spend time pondering. **Give the first, natural answer as it comes to you.** Of course, the questions are too short to give you all the particulars you would sometimes like to have. For instance, the above question asks you about "team games" and you might prefer football to cricket. But you are to reply "for the average game," or to strike an average in situations of the kind stated. Give the best answer you can at a rate not slower than five or six a minute. You should finish in a little more than half an hour.

2.   Try not to fall back on the middle, "uncertain" answers except when the answer at either end is really **impossible** for you – perhaps once every four or five questions.

3.   Be sure not to miss anything out **but answer every question, somehow.** Some may not apply to you very well, but give your best guess. Some may seem personal; but remember that the answer sheets are kept confidential and cannot be scored without a special stencil key. Answers to particular questions are not inspected.

4.   Answer as honestly as possible what is true of you. Do not merely mark what seems "the right thing to say" to impress the examiner.

DO NOT TURN PAGE UNTIL TOLD TO DO SO

Figure 6.3   The 16PF Test

The benefits of group testing can be considerable. Various attributes may be evaluated more easily than in an interview or through other, more abstract tests. In particular, candidates' leadership skills (who are the natural leaders, influencing others and being listened to?), abilities to work as part of a team (who handles others well, being tactful and sensitive to their feelings?) and talents for generating appropriate ideas (whose thoughts are logical and clearly expressed?) are more readily assessed.

However, there are some drawbacks to group testing which must be recognized. It is inappropriate for some groups, especially youngsters who are often too inexperienced to cope with such a sophisticated and directly competitive recruitment technique. Group discussions often grind to a halt after only a few, stuttered comments. Restrict group tests mainly to graduate, supervisory and management positions. It is time-consuming to get all the assessors and candidates together at the same time as well as being costly, bearing in mind the necessary expense of bringing in experts to devise tests and train you to assess candidates properly. The job must therefore be sufficiently important to warrant the financial outlay.

As with all other tests, do not draw up and/or run your own group tests without first seeking and obtaining good, professional advice. You are strongly advised to get in touch with the British Psychological Society or the Institute of Personnel Management (see Appendix C) who will put you in contact with professional experts who can help you.

Summary

Question What role do tests play in the recruitment process?
Answer They should be regarded as an aid, to be used alongside application forms and interviews to create a more complete picture of a candidate.

Question How should tests be carried out?
Answer They should be purchased from a reputable test supplier who will train you to administer and evaluate them properly. Never attempt to design or run them yourself unless you are fully trained and experienced enough.

Question What are general aptitude tests?

Answer   They measure a candidate's basic intelligence. Most people know them as IQ tests.

Question   What are specific aptitude tests?
Answer   They assess a candidate's special talents such as mechanical reasoning or manual dexterity.

Question   What are personality tests?
Answer   As the name implies, they evaluate a candidate's personality so you can establish whether he has the personal qualities required to be a leader, team member and so on.

Question   What are group tests?
Answer   They bring candidates together usually to discuss or deal with a common problem likely to be encountered in the job. Observers watch to see how group members interact with each other.

7 Making a job offer

Having conducted interviews and perhaps tests, you will have decided on the most suitable candidate for the job. You'll now want to know how to offer the job to him, take up references and arrange a medical, if appropriate. Should your job offer be accepted, and assuming any references and medical prove to be satisfactory, you'll then need to reject the remaining, unsuccessful candidates.

Offering the job

Once you have selected your first-choice candidate (and remember to keep a couple of others in reserve in case he turns you down) you can make either an oral or a written offer of employment to him. You'll probably prefer to talk on the telephone so you can promptly ask for permission to approach his referees, discuss when he'll be able to start work and so on. However, bear in mind that this may not always be convenient or acceptable to him, especially if he is currently employed and his employer doesn't know he is job hunting. Also, you could forget to cover all the key points of the offer so that he may start work without fully knowing all that it involves.

It is far better to put a job offer in writing so that everything is set out clearly in black and white, thus avoiding doubts and uncertainties. Your letter ought to contain information concerning:

Dear Mr Jones

Further to our recent meeting, I am pleased to offer you employment as an office assistant at our Head Office. You will be responsible to Mrs Jane Donovan, our office supervisor. This offer is subject to suitable references being received from your referees and the completion of a satisfactory trial period of three months.

Your hours of work will be 9am to 5pm from Monday to Friday inclusive. You will have a one hour lunch break between 1pm and 2pm.

Your salary will be £500 per month, paid on the 15th day of the following month into a bank account of your choice.

You will be entitled to 20 days' paid holiday each year plus statutory holidays. These must be taken in accordance with the staff rota as referred to in the accompanying staff handbook. Our holiday year runs from 6 April to 5 April.

All other terms and conditions of your employment are detailed in the staff handbook which you are asked to read before accepting this offer.

Please confirm within 14 days whether you wish to take up this offer of employment. If so, will you inform me when you will be able to start work and also give me permission to approach your referees.

I look forward to hearing from you.

Yours sincerely

Maureen Reynolds
Sales Manager

Figure 7.1   A written offer of employment

- the job, including the job title, its location, the hours of work, salary, holidays and other information;
- the conditions of the job offer, such as satisfactory references, a medical check up and an acceptable trial period of work;
- a request for written permission to approach referees (wait until this has been received before contacting them);
- the time limit allowed for accepting or rejecting the offer (7–14 days should be sufficient you don't want to delay the recruitment process for too long).

It is a good idea to send a copy of your staff handbook with your written offer. Then the candidate will have the opportunity to fully familiarize himself with all the relevant terms and conditions of employment (including your sickness, disciplinary, grievance, appeal and pension rules and procedures) before starting work.

An example of a written offer of employment is reproduced in Figure 7.1.

Taking up references

Always obtain references before the candidate begins work, but remember not to approach referees until after a job offer has been made and permission has been given by the candidate. References should be regarded as a significant feature of recruitment policy, serving several useful purposes. They allow you to check facts (Is he as experienced as he claims? Does he really earn as much as he says?) and fill in background information about the candidate (Is he friendly and pleasant to work with? Does he fit in well?). It can be difficult to reach the correct selection decision just by studying application forms and holding interviews, and the honest opinions of others who know the chosen candidate and his work well can help to confirm or even overturn it.

Nevertheless, it is best to keep an open mind when reading references. Do not automatically take them at face value. Think carefully about the referees and their possible reasons for making various comments. Personal referees, because they are usually friends or relatives, will typically only praise the candidate, exaggerating his strengths and overlooking weaknesses. As such, they are worthless and should not be requested. Educational referees, form masters, college lecturers and head teachers, see hundreds of students each week and cannot normally be expected to know any of them well enough to assess them fully. In general, only rely on them to verify data about courses taken, exams sat and attendance records. The current employer, who should be approached as the best judge of the candidate's work performance, may be complimentary as he wants to see the candidate leave and save him money. Be sceptical, only being influenced by comments from those referees who are both unbiased and close enough to the candidate to judge him properly.

You can contact referees by letter or telephone. Talking informally over the 'phone is best. A referee will usually be less inhibited and reveal more because he knows his words are off the record – he is unlikely to put unfavourable comments in writing in case the candidate sees them and becomes angry and upset. Telephoning should provide a fuller and more realistic picture of the candidate. Should you wish to telephone, write in advance so that the referee has time to gather his thoughts and knows who you are when you call.

Whether writing or 'phoning, always ask precise questions so that the equally precise answers will enable you to decide if this really is the right person for the job. Vague statements such as 'Tell me all about Mr Jones' and 'Would Mr Jones make a good employee?' will only produce generalized responses as the referee doesn't know exactly what it is you wish to check or discover. Carefully detail the information that you want from the referee ('How long did Mr Jones work for you?' 'In what capacity was he employed?'). If you further expect him to assess the candidate's suitability for the job, tell him what the work involves and the type of person you're looking for, and send him a job description and an employee specification.

In a letter or telephone call to a current or previous employer, you'd probably ask about some or all of the following, with an approach to an educational referee along broadly similar lines:

- the job title
- the job duties and responsibilities
- the length of employment
- pay
- abilities
- conduct
- honesty
- timekeeping and attendance
- health
- reasons for leaving

Selfridges

Oxford Street London W1A 1AB
Telephone 01-629 1234 Telex 24537

Ref: DOJ/2   Personnel Division   Ext. 2304

Dear Sir/Madam,

REFERENCE REQUEST: PRIVATE & CONFIDENTIAL

....

Dates of Employment from .... to ....

Position Held ....

The above named has applied to Selfridges for employment giving
your Company as a previous employer.

We would, therefore, be grateful if you would supply us with a
reference answering the questions detailed below and giving any
additional information you think relevant.

A reply paid envelope is enclosed.

Yours faithfully
FOR SELFRIDGES LIMITED

PERSONNEL DIVISION

Position in Company ....
Date of Employment (Month and Year)
From .... to ....

Salary at the date of leaving ....

Was the person honest? ....

Did this person handle cash? ....

Was this person's attendance and timekeeping satisfactory? ....

Reason for leaving ....

Would you re-employ this person? ....

If not, please state why ....

REMARKS:

Signature .... Position .... Date ....

SELFRIDGES LTD   Registration: England 97117
Registered Office: 400 Oxford Street, London W1A 1AB

Figure 7.2   A letter requesting a reference

Ref: DOJ/5

Dear Sir/Madam,

REFERENCE REQUEST: PRIVATE & CONFIDENTIAL

....

of ....

has applied to us for employment and states that he/she was a

pupil at your School/College from ....

to ....

A pre-paid envelope is enclosed for your reply.

Thanking you in anticipation.

Yours faithfully
FOR SELFRIDGES LIMITED

PERSONNEL DIVISION

1. Are the dates shown above correct YES/NO, if not

    From ....   to ....

2. Would you please give your opinion of the applicant
   in respect of:

    a) Integrity ....

    b) Industry/Application ....

    c) Punctuality & Attendance ....

3. What are his/her strengths? ....

4. What are his/her weaknesses? ....

5. Has he/she held any position of responsibility, e.g. prefect? ....

    ....

6. Details of examination passed ....

    ....

7. Any other comments ....

    ....

    Date .... Signed ....

SELFRIDGES LTD   Registration: England 97117
Registered Office: 400 Oxford Street, London W1A 1AB

Figure 7.3   A letter requesting a reference

- re-employment (enquiring whether the employee would re-employ the candidate will produce a revealing answer).

Examples of letters to referees are given in Figures 7.2 and 7.3, reproduced by courtesy of Selfridges Ltd.

Arranging a medical examination

Satisfactory health is important in any job. You obviously do not wish to employ someone who is continually sick, thus leaving you short-staffed. However, the rigours of the job – the physical demands on an office assistant, store detective and long-distance lorry driver will all differ – should be thought about before you insist on a medical examination as a condition of your job offer. For most jobs, the completion of general health questions on the application form (see Application forms, page 77) and an appropriate reference from a current or former employer should be sufficient.

Where particular medical and/or physical requirements are considered necessary to do the job (and they must be strictly relevant and not introduced simply to eliminate specific groups such as disabled people), you may wish to obtain the medical records of the candidate and/or set up a medical check-up for him. Under the Access to Medical Reports Act 1988, consent to your application for medical information must be gained from the candidate beforehand and forwarded along with your request to the medical practitioner concerned (so, if appropriate, ask for this in your written offer of employment, see Offering the job, page 143).

To arrange a medical, where in-house facilities do not exist, you can contact a local GP who will carry out a straightforward check-up (weight/height ratio, blood pressure and so on) at a relatively low cost (typically £35 to £40 in 1991). Alternatively, if your company has a medical insurance plan for its employees through one of the private health insurance companies such as BUPA or PPP, a full check-up can be arranged at one of their centres (see Appendix C). You, rather than the candidate, should pay for the cost of a medical examination as well as any reasonable travel expenses incurred.

Incidentally, it is worth recalling here that you are obliged by law to have at least 3 per cent of your workforce as registered disabled persons if you employ 20 or more people (see Appendices A and B for further information).

TERMS OF EMPLOYMENT

This is a statement of the main terms and conditions of employment between Gayther and Sons Ltd (the employer) and Timothy Jones (the employee):

Job title: Office Assistant

Job Location: Gayther and Sons Ltd, 9–13 Ravenscroft Industrial Park, Ravenscroft Lane, Whittlesby, Wiltshire

Reports to: The Office Supervisor

Employment commenced: 6 June 1991

Pay: £500 per month, paid on the 15th day of the following month into the employee's bank account.

Hours of work: 35 hours per week, comprising 9am to 5pm Monday to Friday inclusive with a 1-hour lunch break each day between 1pm and 2pm.

Holidays: 20 days' paid holiday per annum plus statutory holidays. The holiday year is from 6 April to 5 April. All holidays must be taken in accordance with the staff rota.

Notice: 2 weeks' notice to be given by the employer for the first 2 years of employment with a further 1 week's notice for every complete year of employment thereafter up to a maximum of 12 weeks notice.
                        2 weeks' notice to be given by the employee, regardless of his length of service.

Figure 7.4   A written statement of the main terms of employment

Figure 7.4 *continued*

> Information concerning the following terms and conditions of employment is given in the staff handbook. A copy is available in the restroom or from your immediate superior.
>
> ● SICKNESS ARRANGEMENTS AND PAY ● PENSION ENTITLEMENTS ● DISCIPLINARY RULES AND PROCEDURES ● GRIEVANCE AND APPEAL RULES AND PROCEDURES.
>
> Employer's signature .... Employee's signature ....
>
> Date .... Date ....

Figure 7.4 *concluded*

Accepting the job

As soon as the candidate has accepted your job offer and all conditions have been met, you must immediately reject the other candidates (see Rejecting candidates, page 152) and start arranging an induction programme to help him to settle into his new role (see Settling in, page 155). Think about drawing up a written statement of the main terms of employment; this is often overlooked.

Under the Employment Protection (Consolidation) Act 1978, a written statement needs to be given to employees who work for 16 hours or more each week within 13 weeks of commencing work. It should also be supplied to those employees who have worked for you for eight hours per week for five years. You will probably want to delay signing it until towards the end of the 13 weeks allowed because your new recruit may be employed on a trial basis up to that stage. Draw it up now so that you can discuss it with him before work begins. He should be aware of all aspects of the job.

A written statement of the main terms of employment, an example of which is reproduced in Figure 7.4, must specify the following:

● the names of the employer and employee

- the date when employment began
- the job title
- the rate and frequency of payment
- the hours of work
- holiday pay and arrangements
- sickness pay and arrangements
- pension entitlement
- notice entitlement and procedures
- disciplinary rules and procedures
- grievance and appeal rules and procedures.

It is usual for especially detailed information, such as disciplinary, grievance and appeal policies, to be supplied in an accompanying staff handbook, to which reference should be made within the written statement.

Rejecting candidates

Your aims when rejecting candidates must be to maintain a caring and friendly company image and to keep on good terms with each of them. They, and their family and friends, may be customers of your company. In addition, they could wish to apply for future vacancies that arise in your company. They will neither buy nor apply again if you have offended them at all.

Contact the candidates as soon as you possibly can to avoid keeping them in suspense for too long. You should be able to tell three or four of the six or so candidates almost immediately after the interview. However, never say no at the end of the interview, or you'll become engaged in a lengthy discussion. Those kept in reserve should be notified once your leading candidate has accepted your offer of employment.

Always write to the unsuccessful candidates rather than telephoning them. A 'phone call may seem more courteous but it often creates additional and unnecessary problems. A candidate's hopes will be raised as he hears your voice and dashed that much harder when you break the bad news to him. If he was extremely keen on the job, and perhaps believed he was going to be offered it, he could become emotional, angrily demanding an explanation. You might become involved in a distressing argument.

When writing, make sure that rejection letters are specifically written to each individual candidate. A 'Dear Sir or Madam' letter – sadly far from uncommon among uncaring companies – shows an appalling lack of thought and interest in the candidates and their feelings. Be certain that names and addresses are spelt correctly, text is polite and your own personal and readable signature is attached. Avoid giving a reason for the rejection. Some candidates will see it as a challenge and may pester you endlessly to insist on further reasons or to attempt to prove you wrong.

Gather all the information you have on the rejected candidates – initial applications, interview and test results, references, any correspondence and so on – and keep it on file for three months. If your new recruit proves to be unsuitable, you may be able to turn to your second- or third-choice candidate instead, assuming, of course, they still think highly enough of your company to want to join it. Bear in mind that dissatisfied candidates who feel they have been discriminated against could decide to complain about you to an industrial tribunal. They have three months in which to do this, so keep records for that length of time to enable you to show you adopted a non-discriminatory recruitment policy.

Dear Mr Johnson

Thank you for attending an interview for the post of office assistant.

We have carefully considered your application but regret to inform you that we are unable to offer you this position.

Thank you for your interest in our company. We wish you every success for the future.

Yours sincerely

Maureen Reynolds
Sales Manager

Figure 7.5 A letter of rejection after an interview

An example of a rejection letter is reproduced in Figure 7.5, by courtesy of Selfridges Ltd.

Summary

Question What procedure ought to be followed once a suitable candidate has been chosen for the job?
Answer   A written offer of employment should be made to your first-choice candidate, while keeping a couple in reserve in case he turns you down or any conditions are not met. Then, take up references and arrange a medical examination, if appropriate. Should your offer be accepted and the references and medical report prove satisfactory, draw up a written statement of the main terms of employment for him. Reject the remaining candidates.

Question Where should references be obtained from?
Answer   Avoid personal references which will be supplied by biased family and friends. Educational references are acceptable only if the teacher or lecturer knows the candidate well. Ask for references from present or former employers who are familiar with the candidate's work rate and performance in an actual job.

Question How can a medical examination be set up?
Answer   If in-house facilities do not exist, contact your local GP or one of the private health insurance companies such as BUPA.

Question What is a written statement of the main terms of employment?
Answer   It is a document detailing the terms and conditions of employment. By law, it must be given to employees, who work for 16 hours or more per week, within 13 weeks of the commencement of employment, and to employees who have worked for eight hours or more each week for five years.

Question How should candidates be rejected?
Answer   A personal and polite letter must be sent to each individual candidate as soon as possible, with the aim of maintaining an image of a pleasant, friendly company. All information about rejected candidates should be kept on file for three months in case a complaint is made to an industrial tribunal.

8 Starting work

The recruitment process must not suddenly end as soon as a job offer is accepted. If recruitment is to be considered successful, you still need to help the new recruit settle down to work for your company on a long-term basis. You should monitor and assess him regularly, developing his strengths and eliminating his weaknesses. You should then review the way you recruited him, learning from your mistakes and making the necessary changes for the future.

Settling in

Induction – the process of settling a recruit into his new job – should serve several purposes. It must fully familiarize him with his role and the company he'll be working for. It should further allow you to get to know him well, recognizing and resolving any problems or special needs he might have. The result will be a happy recruit who wants to stay with you, and he will be able to slot into the workforce swiftly and efficiently. Then, he will start to contribute fully in the shortest possible time.

Induction should have begun early on, and continued throughout the recruitment process. In advertisements, when sending out application forms, during interviews and on making a job offer, you should have constantly been telling the new recruit everything he

155

needs and wants to know. If you've done this, the settling-in period will be much shorter and easier for everybody.

Once the recruit has accepted your offer of employment and you are satisfied that all conditions have been fulfilled, invite him to spend a full day at the company before he starts work. This informal one-day course – make certain you allow enough time as there is much to cover and absorb – will ensure that you can check he is aware of all that is involved in the job. It further enables you to deal with any concerns or queries he may have. Also, you can show him round the premises, introducing him to all relevant departments and fellow employees.

Handle this induction day yourself, promoting a friendly and open image of company management. It's up to you how you approach it but you might typically choose to begin by taking the recruit for a stroll around the building(s). Let him see everyone at work, making a special point of showing him his own department and those he'll be in direct contact with on a regular basis. Indicate where the lavatories, staff room, canteen facilities and so on are as well.

Over a coffee break, talk to the recruit about the job (duties, responsibilities, terms, conditions and so on) and the company (activities, plans, rules, and regulations). Go through the job description, draft written statement of the main terms of employment, staff handbook and any company literature so that everything is clear and totally understood.

Then ask him if he has any uncertainties or doubts that need to be dealt with before he starts work. You may need to ask gently probing questions to elicit information from a shy or nervous person. You could have to be tactful in certain circumstances too. A disabled recruit with limited mobility may feel awkward about requesting a parking space close to the premises. Someone who has to take medication could be embarrassed at mentioning that he wishes to be given the opportunity to do so in privacy.

Attend to any administrative matters at this stage. If you need his bank account details, national insurance number or a P45 from his last employer, ask him to supply this information as soon as possible. Perhaps he can give you what you need on his first day of work.

Introduce the recruit to his immediate superior, workmates and anyone responsible for training him, assuming you have not already done this on your initial walk about the premises. Possibly they could get to know each other over lunch in the staff canteen, if appropriate. Let him sit in and watch them working during the afternoon. Should the former job holder be available, it may be a good idea to get them together to discuss the job, but only if the predecessor is a cheerful person with a positive attitude towards the job and company.

At the end of the induction day, ask if he has any further queries arising from the time spent with you. Remind him to bring in bank account information and so on when he starts work. Thank him for coming and say that you look forward to having him in the team and are always available if he ever has any problems. Warmly bid him goodbye.

Welcome your new employee personally when he arrives to begin his job. Take him along to where he will be working, having made sure beforehand that any desk or cubby hole allocated to him is clean and tidy. Pass him over to his colleagues, having first made certain that they know he is due and will be ready to say 'hallo'. Assign his direct superior or an experienced, sympathetic co-worker to look after him, assisting with his work and dealing with any difficulties that develop. Go and see the employee at lunchtime and at the end of the day to check progress.

Throughout the first couple of weeks – or longer if he seems to be taking time to settle – talk to both the new employee and his immediate superior every day. Discover how well he is doing and try to find out about and resolve any worries. Generally make yourself accessible so that he knows he can turn to you for help and guidance if required.

After a month or so, have an informal talk with the employee to see whether he feels relaxed and comfortable in his job, thinks he needs more guidance and training or has any questions to ask. Speak to his direct superior as well, probing him about the employee's work rate and performance, personality and attitudes, timekeeping and attendance.

Be patient if problems arise – as they tend to – in these early days. Many can be attributed to inexperience (perhaps a youngster is in his first job or a young mother has just returned to work) or a lack of training (possibly 'on-the-job' training needs to be supplemented with external expertise and assistance). Try to give each employee every chance to succeed. Make a firm decision about his future after three months when a formal appraisal should be carried out (see Appraising the new employee, as follows).

Induction may appear to involve excessive time and effort, but it is well worthwhile. A check of company turnover figures will typically reveal that more resignations occur in the first three months of employment than at any other time. This is usually because employees find the job is not what they expected, their concerns are ignored and it is hard to fit into the team. If a little more thought had been put into induction, there would be far fewer resignations and the increasing costs of starting the recruitment process all over again would be avoided.

Appraising the new employee

All employees should be appraised at regular intervals. A new recruit should be formally assessed for the first time after three months, perhaps when his trial period is coming to a close and you have to decide whether to issue a written statement of the main terms of employment. If he is subsequently employed on a permanent basis he would normally then be appraised every six or twelve months, according to circumstances.

Formally assessing staff at regular intervals, in addition to ongoing informal monitoring, offers many benefits. It allows you to identify and encourage an employee's strengths while perhaps recognizing his potential for promotion. It further enables you to illuminate and then work towards rectifying his weaknesses, possibly by providing more training or guidance. Both employer and employee can raise and discuss any issues that may be of mutual concern, such as grievance or disciplinary matters. Knowing he is going to be appraised often will also motivate the employee to work hard and do well.

Staff assessment will usually be carried out during an interview with you, the employee and his immediate superior, if appropriate, all talking about the employee's work performance and progress to date. Agree with the employee beforehand when you'll meet. One or two weeks' notice should be given, thus allowing him enough time to prepare himself. Let him and his direct superior have copies of the assessment form you will be using for appraisal purposes (see below). He'll then know what to expect.

Consider how long the interview should last. Perhaps 30 to 45 minutes need to be set aside if a full assessment is to be carried out. Think about the location of the interview as well. You'll all want to concentrate fully without any distractions. Make certain that you have a quiet and private room available so you can do this (see Timing and location of interviews, page 93).

Prepare for the interview in a systematic way. Draw up a staff assessment form, preferably based on the appropriate job description and employee specification, against which the employee can be appraised. Like application forms, you'll probably need to have three separate ones for youngsters, other employees and managers respectively (see Application forms, page 77).

There are several ways of setting out an assessment form; most companies will use an amalgamation of all of them. Sometimes, the assessor simply has to write out an overall assessment of the employee. It is entirely up to him to decide what he includes or excludes from the form. He comments on those areas he personally considers to be important. Clearly, such an approach has significant drawbacks, not least that it is highly subjective and open to bias.

More often, some guidance will be given, and the assessor will be asked to comment specifically on a range of key criteria of relevance to successful job performance. Although headings will naturally vary according to the type and level of the job concerned, he might typically have to think about the employee's appearance, timekeeping, enthusiasm, reliability, industry and so forth.

As well as providing a brief comment, the assessor may also be expected to grade the employee in each of the various areas. ABCDE or 12345 are most commonly used with A (or 1) perhaps being defined as 'Outstanding work performance and effort', B (or 2) as 'Very satisfactory work performance and effort' and so on. Grading helps to produce a more systematic and thorough analysis of the employee, pinpointing especially good and bad points that should be worked on.

An increasingly popular method of assessment is to set particular targets, perhaps of work performance or output, which the employee must strive to achieve. These would be mutually agreed by both employer and employee on the induction course or at a previous appraisal interview. The review then takes place in comparison with each of these targets.

Whatever your personal choice, the assessment form should also have spaces in which areas for improvement, corresponding actions that need to be taken and employee's observations can be recorded. Always leave plenty of room for each of them. Examples of staff assessment forms, reflecting a variety of approaches, are reproduced in the following pages, by courtesy of the Halifax Building Society, Boots Company Plc and Selfridges Ltd.

Just before the interview, read through the appraisal form, job description, employee specification and any notes made about the employee at the one-month informal review or subsequently if, as

HALIFAX	STAFF PERFORMANCE REVIEW	19	/19

PERSONAL DETAILS

NAME		STAFF No.	
BRANCH/DEPT.		COST CENTRE	
FULL-/PART-TIME		GRADE	
JOB GROUPING		DATE OF REVIEW	

PERFORMANCE ASSESSMENT	Please note that your assessment of performance will directly affect the payment of any performance-related pay award.

	(✔)	RATING
1		**UNSATISFACTORY** Work unacceptable. Needs constant prompting and results are well below the required standard. Makes a significant number of mistakes. Displays little enthusiasm or commitment to work undertaken.
2		**LESS THAN EFFECTIVE** Effort varies. Needs prompting and close supervision. Standard of work requires improvement. Takes few opportunities to produce results and does not willingly tackle demanding work.
3		**EFFECTIVE** Works consistently with little prompting and few delays. Takes most opportunities to produce results and work is of a good standard. Is enthusiastic and committed.
4		**VERY EFFECTIVE** Gets through a great deal of work with minimum supervision. Takes all opportunities to produce results and consistently demonstrates a high level of performance. Displays a high level of enthusiasm, activity and involvement.
5		**OUTSTANDING** Gets through an exceptional amount of work. Actively seeks and takes every opportunity to produce results of an exceptionally high standard. Displays an extremely high level of enthusiasm and total commitment to work undertaken

COMMENTS ON PERFORMANCE

1/9001000-2 (1/90)

Figure 8.1   Staff assessment form

HALIFAX	PERSONAL SKILLS ASSESSMENT

The assessment of Personal Skills is made on the abilities displayed during the review period. It does not affect the payment of any performance-related pay award.

USE THE FOLLOWING SCALE
1 Has significant shortcomings
2 Shows some minor weaknesses
3 Meets the expected performance level
4 Better than would be expected for the current position
5 Displays exceptional ability

SKILL AREA	COMMENTS
A PRODUCT & SERVICES KNOWLEDGE	
Maintains an up-to-date and wide knowledge of the Society's and competitors key products and services.	1 2 3 4 5
B TECHNICAL KNOWLEDGE	
Maintains an up-to-date and wide knowledge of procedures and applies these in an effective manner.	1 2 3 4 5
C COMMUNICATION	
Gives and receives information logically, clearly and concisely both orally and in writing.	1 2 3 4 5
D INITIATIVE	
Generates new or innovative ways of doing things and implements these when appropriate.	1 2 3 4 5
E ACCEPTANCE OF RESPONSIBILITY	
Is willing to accept and able to cope with responsibility whether working alone or with others.	1 2 3 4 5
F ORGANISING ABILITY	
Acts and thinks independently and logically and plans and schedules work to effectively meet deadlines.	1 2 3 4 5
G WILLINGNESS & CAPACITY TO LEARN	
Has the capacity to acquire and retain information quickly and easily being willing to learn in order to gain advancement.	1 2 3 4 5
H ABILITY TO RELATE TO OTHERS	
Projects a self-assured, outgoing manner whilst displaying a sensitivity and being approachable to others.	1 2 3 4 5

Signed: (Assessor)   Date:

Figure 8.1 *continued*

HALIFAX   FURTHER INFORMATION

MOBILITY

1	FULL	— Willing to move home and/or place of work
2	RESTRICTED	— Comments:
3	NONE	

TIMESCALE FOR PROMOTION

Ready Now [1]   Within 12 months [2]   More than 12 months [3]   Not ready [4]

Comments:

OTHER INFORMATION

Current Study Position:-

Recommended for:

[ ] Accelerated Development Selection Board

[ ] Management Development Board

Other (Specify):

DEVELOPMENT PLANS

Figure 8.1 *continued*

Figure 8.1 *concluded*

THE BOOTS COMPANY PLC
PERFORMANCE APPRAISAL

Strictly Confidential

Job Holder	Job Title	Grade or Code	Branch/Territory or Function/Department
		Hay-MSL Job Score	

PERFORMANCE TARGETS FOR 19	PERFORMANCE RATING for each target					REVIEW OF PERFORMANCE AGAINST TARGETS Appraiser's comments to be directly related to the specific Principal Responsibilities and the Job Description
	A	B	C	D	E	

Comments on overall performance	Overall Performance

Please turn over

THIS APPRAISAL HAS BEEN DISCUSSED AND AGREED BETWEEN

Signed _____ APPRAISEE ___/___/___ Date

Signed _____ APPRAISER ___/___/___ Date

Signed _____ REVIEWING MANAGER ___/___/___ Date

OM 72 – 10387

Figure 8.2   Staff assessment form

Starting work 165

TRAINING AND DEVELOPMENT

1. IN-JOB DEVELOPMENT: are any specific actions required to develop performance in the present job and to help meet objectives in the coming year?

2. TRAINING: is training required? Please specify.

3. CAREER ASPIRATIONS: please indicate the job holder's career aspirations both short and long term.

PERFORMANCE RATINGS

A — Exceptionally high performance; this level is likely to be achieved by very few job holders.

B — Superior performance sustained over a period of time, producing results in excess of job demands.

C — Fully acceptable performance. Satisfactory in all major areas of the job.

or Very good progress, but still relatively new in the job (C−, C and C+ may be used if necessary).

D — Performance is unsatisfactory or just about adequate. There are definite areas where improvement should be made.

or Good progress given short time in job.

E — Unacceptable/poor performance

or Performance not yet known (recently appointed with little relevant, previous experience).

If a person is new in the job the prefix 'N' in conjunction with a Performance Rating may be used.

Note: Performance Targets for Next Year. On completing the Appraisal a new form and new targets should be prepared for next year.

Figure 8.2 *concluded*

Selfridges

Management
Appraisal Form

Name:
Position:
Date Appointed to Current Position:
Appraised by:

Figure 8.3   Staff assessment form

TO BE COMPLETED BY THE APPRAISER

Accountability	
Results	**Commentary**
Accountability	
Results	**Commentary**
Accountability	
Results	**Commentary**
Accountability	
Results	**Commentary**
Accountability	
Results	**Commentary**
Accountability	
Results	**Commentary**
Accountability	
Results	**Commentary**

Figure 8.3 *continued*

TO BE COMPLETED BY THE APPRAISER

Key Areas for Performance Improvement in the next year.	How is it planned to achieve these improvements?

TO BE COMPLETED BY THE APPRAISEE

Please comment on your success in achieving Performance Objectives, highlighting major achievements and any areas of difficulty experienced.

Figure 8.3 *continued*

OVERALL PERFORMANCE	TO BE COMPLETED BY THE APPRAISER

Summary of appraisee's overall performance

OVERALL PERFORMANCE (PLEASE TICK)

	Results achieved far exceed job requirements.
	Results achieved consistently exceed job requirements.
	Results achieved meet and sometimes exceed job reqirements.
	Results achieved meet basic requirements.
	Marginal, regular reviews required.

APPRAISEE'S COMMENTS

Indicate your feelings on the appraisal interview and ratings given.

SIGNATURES

Appraisee	Date
Appraiser	Date
Senior Manager or Director	Date

9.89.

Figure 8.3 *continued*

Management Appraisal – Career Development Strategy

Name:	Position:

This section to be completed by the appraisee

How would you like your role to be developed?	
(A) In the short term	(B) In the long term

What assistance would you like to help you achieve your career aims?

Figure 8.3   *continued*

This section to be completed by the appraiser

What factors prevent achievement of these career aims?

Summary of agreed development plan over the next twelve months

Signatures	Appraisee:	Date:
	Appraiser:	Date:

Figure 8.3 *continued*

Management Performance Objectives

Name:	Position:
Date objectives agreed:	Date to be reviewed:

Accountabilities:

Signature:	Date:
Agreed by:	Date:

Figure 8.3 *concluded*

you should, you have been keeping an eye on his progress. Think about the topics you'll be covering and the order in which you'll deal with them. Invariably, you'll choose to adhere closely to the form in front of you, working through each heading in turn.

Begin the interview by helping the employee and, if necessary, his immediate superior to relax. Greet him with a warm smile and a firm handshake. Look at him and use his name. Guide him to his chair, making small talk as appropriate. Once he appears to be at ease, explain the purpose and structure of the interview again. (see Starting an interview, page 96).

Perhaps you could say:

> Thanks for coming in, Tim. Let me run through what we'd like to do. As you know, we appraise all new recruits just before their three-month trial period comes to an end. From the regular chats we've had over that time we have agreed that we're happy with you and vice versa. Nevertheless, it's still a good idea to meet now to talk about progress, see if we have any problems and, if so, how we can work together to eliminate them . . . Okay? . . . Fine, now you've had a couple of weeks to look at our assessment form. As I said when I gave it to you, I'd like to work steadily through the sections with all of us – including you and Mrs Donovan – contributing our thoughts and opinions. Please don't leave me to do all the talking! On agreement, we'll then fill in the form together. Is that all clear, Tim? . . . Good, let's make a start . . .

With a mixture of open and closed questions, encourage the employee to comment first on each particular topic. Try to discover how he sees his strengths and weaknesses and thinks they can be promoted and resolved respectively. Let him tell you about any worries he has and the way in which he views his future with you. Be ready to praise his successes and work constructively through those areas where there is room for improvement. An open and honest exchange of views, bearing in mind you're both on the same side with the identical aim of improving work performance, is highly desirable. (see Questions and answers, page 98).

Conclude by completing the assessment form together. You should then summarize the key points of the interview with particular emphasis on those aspects of the employee's work that need to be attended to, any assistance you have promised to give to help him improve and the mutually agreed targets that must be met by the next assessment. Decide when you'll meet again, typically in six months' time.

Of course, you may feel that the employee is unsuitable for the job and you do not wish to offer him permanent employment once his trial period has finished. Carefully analyse the reasons why this is so. If possible, try to settle any difficulties, perhaps by increasing training or slightly altering job content, as the time and cost involved with starting the recruitment process again are too high to be undertaken lightly. If not, you will reluctantly have to give the employee his notice. An example of a non-continuation of employment letter is given below.

Dear Paul

Further to our meeting this morning, I write to confirm that the company will not be offering you employment once your trial period ends on 6 September. I therefore give you the agreed period of notice of two weeks. You will leave on Friday 6 September.

Will you please come to see me on that day, bringing with you your locker key and any other company items in your possession. Your P45 and final wage packet will be given to you at the same time.

I am sorry that your trial period has not been as successful as we had both hoped. However I wish you every success for the future.

Yours sincerely

Maureen Reynolds
Sales Manager

Figure 8.4   Letter ending employment

However, it is hoped that the new employee will be suitable for the job – he certainly should be if your recruitment process was thorough. Therefore, you would follow up the appraisal interview by confirming permanent employment and issuing the written statement of the main terms of employment (see Figure 7.4). An example of a letter confirming employment is given below.

Dear Tim

I am pleased to confirm your employment as an office assistant following the successful completion of your three-month trial period.

Accordingly, I enclose two copies of your written statement of the main terms of employment. Please sign both of them, keeping one for yourself and returning the other to me for our records.

I am delighted to be able to formally welcome you to our company and hope you will enjoy a long and prosperous career with us.

Yours sincerely

Maureen Reynolds
Sales Manager

Figure 8.5   Letter confirming employment

Summary

Question   How can a new recruit be helped to settle into a job?
Answer   Running a one-day induction course, speaking to him every day for the first two weeks and having an informal talk about his progress after one month are all good ideas. They ought to ensure that he is happy, working well and feels part of the team.

Question   When should a new employee be formally assessed?
Answer   An appraisal interview can be arranged after perhaps three months when a trial period of employment may be coming to an end and a decision needs to be made about his future. All employees ought to be regularly assessed at least once a year.

Question   How must an appraisal interview be carried out?
Answer   The ground rules are the same as for a selection (or any other) interview – find a quiet place, set aside enough time and so on. In addition, the employee should be given a copy of the staff assessment form – detailing the key areas to be evaluated – beforehand so he can study it and prepare himself. This form should be worked through and completed together at the interview.

Question   When does the recruitment process end?
Answer   If a trial period of employment is satisfactorily completed, a written statement of the main terms of employment can be issued. If not, notice must be given and the recruitment programme has to start again. Whatever happens, you also need to look back and review each stage, making improvements for the future.

The recruiter's checklist

A careful and comprehensive approach towards recruitment should ensure that you select the right person for the job, both for now and in the future. Nevertheless, you cannot afford to be complacent. The time and expense of recruiting any new employee, whatever the type and level of job, plus the potential costs of making the wrong choice are immense. Therefore you must constantly review each stage of the recruitment process, identifying and eliminating weaknesses so that future recruitment campaigns run even more smoothly and efficiently.

For recruitment to be successful, you need to adhere closely to a sequence of separate steps. They can be grouped together under the following (chapter) headings:

- Planning staff requirements
- Seeking applicants
- Attracting applicants
- Screening applicants
- Interviewing candidates
- Testing candidates
- Making a job offer
- Starting work

Planning staff requirements

- Think carefully about the job which has become vacant. It may need to be updated in some way.
- Consider the type of person required to do the job. He could be totally dissimilar to the current job holder.
- Conduct a thorough job analysis. Make any necessary alterations to the job.
- Draw up a job description. Refer to it at all times.

- Draft an employee specification. Use it throughout the recruitment process.
- Prepare a manpower plan. Recruit staff on the basis of future needs.

Seeking applicants

- Weigh up the benefits and drawbacks of internal and external recruitment. Decide whether to recruit internally or externally.
- Study the various internal and external sources of recruitment available. Use those which reach the right type and number of people at the right price.
- Continually measure and assess the response from each selected source of recruitment. Implement changes as desired.

Attracting applicants

- Design recruitment advertisements which will encourage a compact pool of quality applicants to apply for the job.
- Base all advertisements on the job description and employee specification. Prospective applicants will then be able to tell if they are suitable for the company and job, and vice versa.
- Create advertisements which are eye-catching to attract attention. Make certain they are also concise, logical, humour-free and non-discriminatory to retain interest.
- Regularly monitor and evaluate the feedback from each advertisement. Adjust as required.

Screening applicants

- Analyse the screening methods most commonly used to compile a shortlist of candidates. Choose one which is appropriate to individual circumstances.
- If relevant, compose an application form from the job description and employee specification, posing the right questions in the right order. It should be short and concise too.
- Acknowledge all applications on receipt. This will convey a caring company image.

- Compare applications with the employee specification, inviting suitable applicants in for an interview. Unsuitable ones ought to be rejected in a prompt and pleasant manner.

Interviewing candidates

- Arrange to conduct selection interviews in a quiet, uninterrupted room. Allow plenty of time to exchange information.
- If possible, greet candidates personally on arrival. Be sure they are relaxed before questioning begins.
- Run interviews according to an interview plan, dealing with various topics and questions in turn. Adapt it when necessary.
- Let candidates ask questions at the end of the interview. Answer them fully and honestly.
- Conclude by saying when a decision will be made. Signal the interview is over by standing up and bidding the candidate farewell.
- Collect together all the accumulated details about each candidate. Look at them in relation to the employee specification, subsequently selecting the most suitable one.

Testing candidates

- If needed, set up tests as an aid to reaching a selection decision. Use them only if information cannot be accurately obtained in other ways.
- Think about the types of test available – general aptitude, specific aptitude, personality and group. Pick those which will enable comparisons to be made with the key criteria on the employee specification.
- Buy tests from reputable test suppliers. Undergo full training before administering and evaluating them.

Making a job offer

- Make a written offer of employment to the first choice candidate. Hold second- and third-choice candidates in reserve in case of rejection or unsatisfactory references or medical examination.

- Take up references, preferably from present and former employers. Avoid personal references.
- If appropriate, arrange a medical examination for the candidate. This can be carried out by a local GP or through a private health insurance company.
- On acceptance of the job offer, and assuming all conditions are met, prepare a written statement of the main terms of employment. Sign it once a trial period has been satisfactorily completed.
- Reject remaining candidates in a fair and friendly manner. Keep applications on file for three months in case of complaint to an industrial tribunal.

Starting work

- Set up a one-day induction course for the new recruit before he starts work. This will help everyone to get to know each other better.
- Monitor the recruit's progress every day for the first few weeks of employment. Conduct an informal assessment after one month.
- Formally appraise the new employee after three months, confirming or ending employment. Run further appraisal interviews every six or twelve months thereafter if he is retained.
- Review the recruitment process. Make improvements for forthcoming recruitment programmes.

Appendix A
Avoiding discrimination: the law

If you are to avoid discriminating because of sex, marital status, race and disability, you need to be aware of the key points of these acts:

- The Sex Discrimination Act 1975
- The Race Relations Act 1976
- The Disabled Persons (Employment) Acts 1944 and 1958.

The Sex Discrimination Act 1975

1. It is unlawful to discriminate on the grounds of sex or marital status with regard to the arrangements made for filling a job vacancy, deciding who should be given the job and the terms of employment offered.
2. Employees – whatever their sex or marital status – are entitled to equal access (on equal terms) to training, transfer, promotion and any other facilities, services and benefits available. They must not be subjected to sexual harassment or be discriminated against when staff have to be selected for redundancy. Neither should they be dismissed nor receive any other unfavourable treatment for discriminatory reasons.
3. Unlawful discrimination may be termed either 'direct' or 'indirect'. Direct discrimination occurs when one person is treated less favourably than another (of the opposite sex or marital status) or would be treated in the same (or similar) circumstances. Indirect discrimination exists when requirements or conditions are set which, although they may appear fair, tend to favour people of one sex or marital status more than another.
4. The Act applies to women *and* men, full time *and* part-time

181

employees, self-employed people contracted to do work and pregnant women, regardless of their length of employment. No minimum period of employment is needed for this Act to be effective.

5. There are some exceptions to the Act. Sex discrimination is lawful in recruitment, training and access to transfer or promotion if it is a 'genuine occupational qualification' for the job. A person of a particular sex may be required for authenticity, to preserve privacy or decency, when the organization provides care and attention for people of only one sex or where the job involves the provision of personal services promoting education or welfare which is best supplied by one sex.

6. Other exceptions relate to certain jobs in private households, the Army, Navy, Air Force, prison service and police force. Further advice, and guidance on any other specific matters, can be obtained from The Equal Opportunities Commission (see *Appendix C*).

The Race Relations Act 1976

1. It is illegal to discriminate because of colour, race, nationality or ethnic origins in the field of employment. The Act applies to all employers and employment circumstances from recruitment through to dismissal and redundancy situations. All racial groups have a right to equal opportunity at all times.

2. Direct discrimination consists of treating a person of one racial group less favourably than another would be treated in the same circumstances. Indirect discrimination involves setting conditions or requirements which favour one racial group more than another.

3. The Act does not cover employment in a private household or the civil service. Selection on racial grounds is allowed in jobs where it is a genuine occupational qualification (for reasons of authenticity and so on).

4. The Commission for Racial Equality is dedicated to eliminating racial discrimination and promoting equality of opportunity and good race relations. They should be approached if more information is required. (see *Appendix C*).

The Disabled Persons (Employment) Acts 1944 and 1958

1. Under the 1944 Act (amended by the 1958 Act), a voluntary register of people with disabilities was set up. Employers with 20 or more employees have a duty to employ a quota of these registered disabled people. The quota currently stands at 3 per cent of the total workforce.
2. Although it is not an offence to be below quota, such an employer has a responsibility to take on suitable registered disabled people if they are available as and when vacancies occur. If he wants to recruit someone else, he must obtain a permit to do so from his local job centre. Also, he should not dismiss a registered disabled person without reasonable cause if he is below quota (or will become so as a consequence of the dismissal).
3. The Act also includes the power to reserve various jobs for registered disabled people. Under the Designated Employments Scheme, the occupations of car park attendant and passenger electric lift attendant are reserved for people with disabilities.
4. Employers who have over 20 employees and/or who have designated employments have to keep records showing the number and names of people employed with their starting (and finishing) dates of employment. These records must identify registered disabled people, those employed under a permit and/or in designated employment.
5. Helpful advice about this law – and any other aspects of employing disabled people – may be obtained from the Department of Employment's Disablement Advisory Service (see *Appendix C*).

To ensure that you do not discriminate on the grounds of sex, marital status, race and disability, you should follow the codes of practice issued by the Equal Opportunities Commission, The Commission for Racial Equality and The Department of Employment. Key extracts from each of these codes follow in Appendix B, reproduced by courtesy of these organizations.

Appendix B
Avoiding discrimination:
the codes of practice

The Equal Opportunities Commission:
Code of Practice*

RECRUITMENT

12. It is unlawful: UNLESS THE JOB IS COVERED BY AN EXCEPTION TO DISCRIMINATE DIRECTLY OR INDIRECTLY ON THE GROUNDS OF SEX OR MARRIAGE
    - IN THE ARRANGEMENTS MADE FOR DECIDING WHO SHOULD BE OFFERED A JOB
    - IN ANY TERMS OF EMPLOYMENT
    - BY REFUSING OR OMITTING TO OFFER A PERSON EMPLOYMENT

13. It is therefore recommended that:
    (a) each individual should be assessed according to his or her personal capability to carry out a given job. It should not be assumed that men only or women only will be able to perform certain kinds of work;
    (b) any qualifications or requirements applied to a job which effectively inhibit applications from one sex or from married people should be retained only if they are justifiable in terms of the job to be done;

* Extract reproduced by kind permission of the Equal Opportunities Commission.

(c) any age limits should be retained only if they are necessary for the job. An unjustifiable age limit could constitute unlawful indirect discrimination, for example, against women who have taken time out of employment for child-rearing;

(d) where trade unions uphold such qualifications or requirements as union policy, they should amend that policy in the light of any potentially unlawful effect.

GENUINE OCCUPATIONAL QUALIFICATIONS (GOQs)

14. It is unlawful: EXCEPT FOR CERTAIN JOBS WHEN A PERSON'S SEX IS A GENUINE OCCUPATIONAL QUALIFICATION (GOQ) FOR THAT JOB to select candidates on the ground of sex.

15. There are very few instances in which a job will qualify for a GOQ on the ground of sex. However, exceptions may arise, for example, where considerations of privacy and decency or authenticity are involved. The SDA expressly states that the need of the job for strength and stamina does not justify restricting to men. When a GOQ exists for a job, it applies also to promotion, transfer, or training for that job, but cannot be used to justify a dismissal.

16. In some instances, the GOQ will apply to some of the duties only. A GOQ will not be valid, however, where members of the appropriate sex are already employed in sufficient numbers to meet the employer's likely requirements without undue inconvenience. For example, in a job where sales assistants may be required to undertake changing room duties, it might not be lawful to claim a GOQ in respect of *all* the assistants on the grounds that any of them might be required to undertake changing room duties from time to time.

17. It is therefore recommended that:
    – A job for which a GOQ was used in the past should be re-examined if the post falls vacant to see whether the GOQ still applies. Circumstances may well have changed, rendering the GOQ inapplicable.

SOURCES OF RECRUITMENT

18. It is unlawful: UNLESS THE JOB IS COVERED BY AN EXCEPTION:

    – TO DISCRIMINATE ON GROUNDS OF SEX OR MARRIAGE IN THE ARRANGEMENTS MADE FOR DETERMINING WHO SHOULD BE OFFERED EMPLOYMENT WHETHER RECRUITING BY ADVERTISEMENTS, THROUGH EMPLOYMENT AGENCIES, JOBCENTRES, OR CAREER OFFICES.

    – TO IMPLY THAT APPLICATIONS FROM ONE SEX OR FROM MARRIED PEOPLE WILL NOT BE CONSIDERED.

    – TO INSTRUCT OR PUT PRESSURE ON OTHERS TO OMIT TO REFER FOR EMPLOYMENT PEOPLE OF ONE SEX OR MARRIED PEOPLE UNLESS THE JOB IS COVERED BY AN EXCEPTION.

    It is also unlawful WHEN ADVERTISING JOB VACANCIES,

    – TO PUBLISH OR CAUSE TO BE PUBLISHED AN ADVERTISEMENT WHICH INDICATES OR MIGHT REASONABLY BE UNDERSTOOD AS INDICATING AN INTENTION TO DISCRIMINATE UNLAWFULLY ON GROUNDS OF SEX OR MARRIAGE.

19. It is therefore recommended that:

Advertising

(a) job advertising should be carried out in such a way to encourage applications from suitable candidates of both sexes. This can be achieved both by wording of the advertisements and, for example, by placing advertisements in publications likely to reach both sexes. All advertising material and accompanying literature relating to employment or training issues should be reviewed to ensure that it avoids presenting men and women in stereotyped roles. Such stereotyping tends to perpetuate sex segregation in jobs and can also lead people of the opposite sex to believe that they would be unsuccessful in applying for particular jobs;

(b) where vacancies are filled by promotion or transfer, they should be published to all eligible employees in such a way that they do not restrict applications from either sex;

(c) recruitment solely or primarily by word of mouth may unnecessarily restrict the choice of applicants available. The method should be avoided in a workforce predominantly of one sex, if in practice it prevents members of the opposite sex from applying;

(d) where applicants are supplied through trade unions and members of one sex only come forward, this should be discussed with the unions and an alternative approach adopted.

Careers Service/Schools

20. When notifying vacancies to the Careers Service, employers should specify that these are open to both boys and girls. This is especially important when a job has traditionally been done exclusively or mainly by one sex. If dealing with single sex schools, they should ensure, where possible, that both boys' and girls' schools are approached; it is also a good idea to remind mixed schools that jobs are open to boys and girls.

SELECTION METHODS

Tests

21. (a) If selection tests are used, they should be specifically related to job and/or career requirements and should measure an individual's actual or inherent ability to do or train for the work or career.

(b) Tests should be reviewed regularly to ensure that they remain relevant and free from any unjustifiable bias, either in content or in scoring mechanism.

Applications and Interviewing

22. It is unlawful: UNLESS THE JOB IS COVERED BY AN EXCEPTION:

TO DISCRIMINATE ON GROUNDS OF SEX OR MARRIAGE BY REFUSING OR DELIBERATELY OMITTING TO OFFER EMPLOYMENT.

23. It is therefore recommended that:

(a) employers should ensure that personnel staff, line managers and all other employees who may come into contact with job applicants, should be trained in the provisions of the SDA, including the fact that it is unlawful to instruct or put pressure on others to discriminate;

(b) applications from men and women should be processed in exactly the same way. For example, there should not be separate lists of male and female or married and single applicants. All those handling applications and conducting interviews should be trained in the avoidance of unlawful discrimination and records of interviews kept, where practicable, showing why applicants were or were not appointed;

(c) questions should relate to the requirements of the job. Where it is necessary to assess whether personal circumstances will affect performance of the job (for example, where it involves unsocial hours or extensive travel) this should be discussed objectively without detailed questions based on assumptions about marital status, children and domestic obligations. Questions about marriage plans or family intentions should not be asked, as they could be construed as showing bias against women. Information necessary for personnel records can be collected after a job offer has been made.

PROMOTION, TRANSFER AND TRAINING

24. It is unlawful: UNLESS THE JOB IS COVERED BY AN EXCEPTION, FOR EMPLOYERS TO DISCRIMINATE DIRECTLY OR INDIRECTLY ON THE GROUND OF SEX OR MARRIAGE IN THE WAY THEY AFFORD ACCESS TO OPPORTUNITIES FOR PROMOTION, TRANSFER OR TRAINING.

25. It is therefore recommended that:

(a) where an appraisal system is in operation, the assessment criteria should be examined to ensure that they are not unlawfully discriminatory and the scheme monitored to assess how it is working in practice;

(b) when a group of workers predominantly of one sex is excluded from an appraisal scheme, access to promotion, transfer and training and to other benefits should be reviewed, to ensure that there is no unlawful indirect discrimination;

(c) promotion and career development patterns are reviewed to ensure that the traditional qualifications are justifiable requirements for the job to be done. In some circumstances, for example, promotion on the basis of length of service could amount to unlawful indirect discrimination, as it may unjustifiably affect more women than men;

(d) when general ability and personal qualities are the main requirements for promotion to a post, care should be taken to consider favourably candidates of both sexes with differing career patterns and general experience;

(e) rules which restrict or preclude transfer between certain jobs should be questioned and changed if they are found to be unlawfully discriminatory. Employees of one sex may be concentrated in sections from which transfers are traditionally restricted without real justification;

(f) policies and practices regarding selection for training, day release and personal development should be examined for unlawful direct and indirect discrimination. Where there is found to be an imbalance in training as between sexes, the cause should be identified to ensure that it is not discriminatory;

(g) age limits for access to training and promotion should be questioned.

The Commission for Racial Equality: Code of Practice*

Recruitment, promotion, transfer, training & dismissal

Sources of Recruitment

Advertisements

1.5 *When advertising job vacancies it is unlawful for employers:*

to publish an advertisement which indicates, or could reasonably be understood as indicating, an intention to discriminate against applicants from a particular racial group.

1.6 It is therefore recommended that:

a) employers should not confine advertisements unjustifiably to those areas or publications which would exclude or disproportionately reduce the numbers of applicants of a particular racial group;

b) employers should avoid prescribing requirements such as length of residence or experience in the UK and where a particular qualification is required it should be made clear that a fully comparable qualification obtained overseas is as acceptable as a UK qualification.

1.7 In order to demonstrate their commitment to equality of opportunity it is recommended that where employers send literature to applicants, this should include a statement that they are equal opportunity employers.

Employment Agencies

1.8 *When recruiting through employment agencies, job centres, careers offices and schools, it is unlawful for employers:*

* Extract reproduced with kind permission of the Commission for Racial Equality.

a) to give instructions to discriminate, for example by indicating that certain groups will or will not be preferred. (For exceptions see the Race Relations Act);

b) to bring pressure on them to discriminate against members of a particular racial group. (For exceptions, as above).

1.9 In order to avoid indirect discrimination it is recommended that employers should not confine recruitment unjustifiably to those agencies, job centres, careers offices and schools which, because of their particular source of applicants, provide only or mainly applicants of a particular racial group.

Other Sources

1.10 *It is unlawful to use recruitment methods which exclude or disproportionately reduce the numbers of applicants of a particular racial group and which cannot be shown to be justifiable.* It is therefore recommended that employers should not recruit through the following methods:

a) recruitment, solely or in the first instance, through the recommendations of existing employees where the workforce concerned is wholly or predominantly white or black and the labour market is multi-racial;

b) procedures by which applicants are mainly or wholly supplied through trade unions where this means that only members of a particular racial group, or a disproportionately high number of them, come forward.

Sources for Promotion and Training

1.11 *It is unlawful for employers to restrict access to opportunities for promotion or training in a way which is discriminatory.* It is therefore recommended that:

– job and training vacancies and the application procedure should be made known to all eligible employees, and not in such a way as to exclude or disproportionately reduce the numbers of applicants from a particular racial group.

Selection for recruitment, promotion, transfer, training and dismissal

1.12 *It is unlawful to discriminate,* not only in recruitment, promotion, transfer and training, but also in the arrangements made for recruitment and in the ways of affording access to opportunities for promotion, transfer or training.*

Selection Criteria and Tests

1.13 In order to avoid direct or indirect discrimination it is recommended that selection criteria and tests are examined to ensure that they are related to job requirements and are not unlawfully discriminatory. For example:

a) a standard of English higher than that needed for the safe and effective performance of the job or clearly demonstrable career pattern should not be required, or a higher level of educational qualification than is needed;

b) in particular, employers should not disqualify applicants because they are unable to complete an application form unassisted unless personal completion of the form is a valid test of the standard of English required for safe and effective performance of the job;

c) overseas degrees, diplomas and other qualifications which are comparable with UK qualifications should be accepted as equivalents, and not simply be assumed to be of an inferior quality;

d) selection tests which contain irrelevant questions or exercises on matters which may be unfamiliar to racial minority applicants should not be used (for example, general knowledge questions on matters more likely to be familiar to indigenous applicants);

e) selection tests should be checked to ensure that they are related to the job's requirements, i.e. an individual's test markings should measure ability to do or train for the job in question.

* It should be noted that discrimination in selection to achieve 'racial balance' is not allowed. The clause in the 1968 Race Relations Act which allowed such discrimination for the purpose of securing or preserving a reasonable balance of persons of different racial groups in the establishment is not included in the 1976 Race Relations Act.

Treatment of Applicants, Shortlisting, Interviewing and Selection

1.14 In order to avoid direct or indirect discrimination it is recommended that:

   a) gate, reception and personnel staff should be instructed not to treat casual or formal applicants from particular racial groups less favourably than others. These instructions should be confirmed in writing;

   b) in addition, staff responsible for shortlisting, interviewing and selecting candidates should be:

   – clearly informed of selection criteria and of the need for their consistent application;

   – given guidance or training on the effects which generalised assumptions and prejudices about race can have on selection decisions;

   – made aware of the possible misunderstandings that can occur in interviews between persons of different cultural background;

   c) wherever possible, shortlisting and interviewing should not be done by one person alone but should at least be checked at a more senior level.

Genuine Occupational Qualification

1.15 *Selection on racial grounds is allowed in certain jobs where being of a particular group is a genuine occupational qualification for that job.* An example is where the holder of a particular job provides persons of a racial group with personal services promoting their welfare, and those services can most effectively be provided by a person of that group.

Transfers and Training

1.16 In order to avoid direct or indirect discrimination it is recommended that:

   a) staff responsible for selecting employees for transfer to other jobs should be instructed to apply section criteria without unlawful discrimination;

b) industry or company agreements and arrangements of custom and practice on job transfers should be examined and amended if they are found to contain requirements or conditions which appear to be indirectly discriminatory. For example, if employees of a particular racial group are concentrated in particular sections, the transfer arrangements should be examined to see if they are unjustifiably and unlawfully restrictive and amended if necessary;

c) staff responsible for selecting employees for training, whether induction, promotion or skill training should be instructed not to discriminate on racial grounds;

d) selection criteria for training opportunities should be examined to ensure that they are not indirectly discriminatory.

The Department of Employment: Code of Good Practice on the Employment of Disabled People*

Recruiting People with Disabilities – The Recruitment and Selection Process*

5.1 If people with disabilities are to obtain opportunities within your company according to their abilities, then it is important that you use recruitment methods which encourage applicants with disabilities. It is also important to ensure that your application and selection procedures do not discourage or exclude people with disabilities because they have a disability. This section describes some ways of ensuring that you attract applications from suitable people with disabilities and that your application and selection procedures are fair to these workers.

Job descriptions and job requirements

5.2 Whatever your recruitment methods, remember when drawing up job descriptions that certain job requirements may inadvertently exclude people with disabilities more so than other applicants. It is therefore important to check that job requirements are strictly related to the needs of the job. For instance, avoid where possible the setting of unnecessarily rigid age limits as unemployed people with disabilities tend to be older than other workers. Where job requirements are flexible, make this clear in the job description. For example, to require applicants to have a driving licence when the ability to drive is only occasionally useful rather than essential could well exclude some suitable applicants with disabilities, e.g. blind people.

Methods of recruitment – ways of encouraging suitable people with disabilities to apply for your jobs

5.3 Your company will have sources of recruitment appropriate to its own needs. However, if the number of people with disabilities it employs is to increase, you will need to know of the methods

* Extracts from the Code reproduced with kind permission of the Department of Employment Group.

of recruitment well placed to put you in touch with people with disabilities interested in your vacancies. These are:

- staff at your local Jobcentre, including the Disablement Resettlement Officer;
- the specialist careers officer or other staff at your local careers office;
- special schools, or special units for people with disabilities within ordinary schools. Consider building links with these. A good example is a firm making high precision instruments which, in a workforce of 100, employs 20 people with disabilities. Most of these were recruited from a local special school and some have been with the firm for over 20 years;
- organisations for people with disabilities in your area;
- other organisations which can put you in touch with suitable candidates with disabilities.

Advertising vacancies in the press

5.4 If your company advertises vacancies in the press, a short statement in the advertisement that applications from people with disabilities are welcome will:

- help to ensure that your company is recognised as one which offers fair opportunities to people with disabilities;
- encourage suitable workers with disabilities to apply.

Other methods of recruitment

5.5 If you use other methods of recruitment, such as private agencies or informal contacts, let it be known that applications from people with disabilities are welcome.

Application and selection procedures

5.6 The aim of any selection process will be to ensure that you get the right people for the job. To do that you will look at their abilities, experience and likely commitment. This is exactly what you should do for applicants with disabilities. However, you will also need to know about any disability which is relevant to the job in question. This will help you to make a full assessment and to consider whether any special help is needed.

5.7 Many people with disabilities are quite prepared to give details of their disability. Others may be unwilling to divulge such information for a number of reasons:

- they believe the disability has no effect on ability to do the job in question and is thus not relevant to the job application;
- there may be a fear that if a disability which is not immediately apparent is revealed (eg. a history of epileptic attacks at work) an interview will not be granted, irrespective of ability to do the job.

5.8 It is therefore important for your company to consider carefully the circumstances in which it needs to know about any disability and the use it makes of this information. You will do much to reassure workers with disabilities if you make it clear on application forms, during interviews or in connection with health screening and medical checks that disability does not preclude full consideration for the job.

Application forms

5.9 Give some extra thought to the wording of application forms – a considerable amount of professional personnel expertise exists in this field. A positive approach would be to preface any questions about health or disability with a statement that the company welcomes applications from suitable people with disabilities and that all information is treated as confidential.

5.10 An example of an appropriately worded statement is:
a disability or health problem does not preclude full consideration for the job and applications from suitable people with disabilities are welcome. All information provided by applicants will be treated as confidential.

5.11 Examples of appropriately worded questions are:–

1. *Do you have a health problem, or a disability, which is relevant to our job application?*

2. *If yes, please describe the health problem or disability in this space.*

3. *If yes, are you registered as disabled with the Jobcentre (do you hold a green card)?*

5.12 Where your company has access to occupational medical or nursing advice, detailed questioning on health may need to be covered in a separate health questionnaire. This should be seen only by occupational health staff and relevant information it contains given only to personnel, managerial or supervisory staff concerned with the application.

Interviewing candidates

5.13 Application forms often only give simplified information and a brief picture. The only realistic and effective means of assessing the employment potential of workers with disabilities may be through interviews. You should consider therefore inviting all suitably qualified candidates with disabilities for interview, particularly if your company employs only a small number of people with disabilities or does not fulfill quota.

Practical interview arrangements

5.14 In the case of some people with disabilities, special arrange-ments for interviews may be needed and, where appropriate, invitations to interview could ask if this is the case. Examples of such arrangements are:

- allowing deaf or speech-impaired people to bring an inter-preter if they wish (a special service exists which can arrange for an interpreter)
- alerting staff to be prepared to show blind people to the place of interview;
- allowing mentally handicapped people to bring a friend or relative to assist when answering questions;
- ensuring that the place of interview is accessible to any candidate with a mobility problem, or that assistance is available to help them on arrival.

5.15 In addition to the normal preparations which you make for interviewing all workers, it may be helpful to gain some prior knowledge of any disability and possible handicap which may have to be discussed. If the candidate has been referred by jobcentre staff, then they may be able to give you relevant information. The Employers Guide to Disabilities, published by Woodhead Faulkner in conjunction with the Royal Association for Disability and Rehabilitation provides concise and helpful information.

The interview itself

5.16 Most candidates at interviews are likely to be nervous. People with disabilities particularly so because of past experiences where they consider employers had been unable to look beyond their disabilities. Try, therefore, to put candidates with disabilities more at their ease by emphasising that disability does not affect the consideration they will receive. You will of course want to discuss any possible handicap fully and objectively, but do not make assumptions about what a candidate with a disability, for instance someone with a physical handicap, can or cannot do. The interview should concentrate on the person's abilities and if possible provide an opportunity for these to be demonstrated, e.g. manual dexterity.

Health screening

5.17 Health checks, whether short health screening checks or full medical examinations, are by no means necessary in the case of all jobs, nor are they necessary in the case of all people with disabilities. Your company will no doubt have its own policy with regard to health screening, and people with disabilities should be considered in the same way as other people within that policy.

5.18 People with disabilities should not be excluded from jobs because it is thought that health screening will automatically lead to their rejection.

5.19 However, it is important also that you do not reject a candidate with a disability on the basis of doubts about such things as fitness, safety or the severity of a handicap when health checks or a medical examination could dispel such doubts. If you need advice, the Employment Medical Advisory Service of the Health and Safety Executive will advise you on the desirability of health checks in particular instances before employment is offered and has published a guidance note on pre-employment health screening.

The Job Introduction Scheme

5.20 If you are still unsure about a disabled worker's ability to do a particular job, ask the local Jobcentre about the Job Introduction Scheme. This Scheme provides financial assistance through the Employment Service to enable you to take a worker with a disability on trial.

5.21 Similar assistance is also available through the Pathway Scheme run by the Royal Society for Mentally Handicapped Children and Adults (MENCAP). This Scheme, which runs alongside the Job Introduction Scheme, is gradually being introduced nation-wide. It provides grants to the employer and to a fellow worker to encourage the recruitment and training of mentally handi-capped people.

Appendix C   Sources of advice

These organizations provide help and guidance with various aspects of staff recruitment.

British Institute of Management, Management House, Cottingham Road, Corby, Northants NN17 ITT (0536 204222)

British Psychological Society, St Andrew's House, 48 Princess Road East, Leicester LE1 7DR (0533 549568)

BUPA Medical Centre Ltd, Webb House, 210 Pentonville Road, London W1 (071 837 8641)

Commission for Racial Equality, Elliot House, 10–12 Allington Street, London SW1E 5EH (071 828 7022)

Disablement Advisory Service, through your local job centre

Employment Service, Steel City House, Moorfoot, Sheffield S1 4PQ (0742 739190)

Equal Opportunities Commission, Overseas House, Quay Street, Manchester M3 3HN (061 833 9244).

Executive Recruitment Association, 36–38 Mortimer Street, London W1N 7RB (071 323 4300).

Federation of Recruitment and Employment Services Ltd, 36–38 Mortimer Street, London W1N 7RB (071 323 4300).

Health and Safety Executive, Baynards House, 1 Chepstow Place, London W2 4TC (071 229 3456)

Institute of Employment Consultants, 6 Guildford Road, Woking, Surrey GU22 7PX (0483 766442)

Institute of Management Consultants, 32 Hatton Garden, London EC1N 8DJ (071 242 2140)

Institute of Personnel Management, IPM House, Camp Road, Wimbledon, London SW19 4UX (081 946 9100)

Management Consultancies Association Ltd, 11 West Halkin Street, London SW1X 8JL (071 235 3897)

NFER-Nelson, Darville House, 2 Oxford Road East, Windsor, Berkshire SL4 1DF (0753 850333)

Open University, Walton Hall, Milton Keynes, Bucks MK7 6BN (0908 653449)

Opportunities for the Disabled, 1 Bank Buildings, Princes Street, London EC2R 8EU (071 726 4961)

Oracle Teletext Ltd, Craven House, 25–32 Marshall Street, London W1V 1LL (071 434 3121)

PPP Medical Centre, 99 New Cavendish Street, London W1M 3FQ (071 637 8941)

Royal Association for Disability and Rehabilitation, 25 Mortimer Street, London W1N 8AB (071 637 5400)

Appendix D   Further reading

The following books are highly recommended. You should be able to obtain them from your local library or bookshop. Alternatively, contact the appropriate publisher.

Anastasi, A., *Psychological Testing*, Collier Macmillan, London, 1982.

Birkett, K. and Worman, D., *Getting On With Disabilities, An Employer's Guide*, Institute of Personnel Management, London, 1988.

Bolton, G.M., *Testing in Selection Decisions*, NFER-Nelson, Windsor, 1983.

Fletcher, J., *Effective Interviewing*, Kogan Page, London, 1988.

Goodworth, C., *The Secrets of Successful Staff Appraisal and Counselling*, Heinemann, Oxford, 1989.

Payne, D. and MacKenzie K., *Employment Contract Manual*, Gower, Aldershot, 1987.

Pearn, M. and Kandola, R., *Job Analysis: A Practical Guide for Managers*, Institute of Personnel Management, London, 1988.

Rae, L., *The Skills of Interviewing*, Gower, Aldershot, 1988.

Ray, M., *Recruitment Advertising*, Institute of Personnel Management, London, 1980.

Rodger, A. and Rawling, K., *The Seven Point Plan*, NFER-Nelson, Windsor, 1985.

Thompson, M., *Employment for Disabled People*, Kogan Page, London, 1986.

Toplis, J., Dulewicz V. and Fletcher, C., *Psychological Testing: A Practical Guide*, Institute of Personnel Management, London, 1987.

Ungerson, B., *How to Write a Job Description*, Institute of Personnel Management, London 1983.

Index

SPIKE & THE SMUGGLERS

by

DEBORAH VAN DER BEEK

Illustrated by the author

HAMISH HAMILTON
LONDON

0064387708

HAMISH HAMILTON LTD

Published by the Penguin Group
27 Wrights Lane, London w8 5tz, England
Penguin Books USA Inc., 375 Hudson Street, New York, New York 10014, USA
Penguin Books Australia Ltd, Ringwood, Victoria, Australia
Penguin Books Canada Ltd, 10 Alcorn Avenue, Toronto, Ontario, Canada m4v 3b2
Penguin Books (NZ) Ltd, 182–190 Wairau Road, Auckland 10, New Zealand

Penguin Books Ltd, Registered Offices: Harmondsworth, Middlesex, England

First published in Great Britain 1992 by Hamish Hamilton Ltd

Copyright © 1992 by Deborah van der Beek
Illustrations copyright © 1992 by Deborah van der Beek

1 3 5 7 9 10 8 6 4 2

The moral right of the author has been asserted

British Library Cataloguing in Publication Data
CIP data for this book is available from the British Library

ISBN 0-241-13175-8

Set in 15pt Baskerville by Rowland Phototypesetting Ltd
Bury St Edmunds, Suffolk
Printed and bound in Great Britain by
BPCC Hazell Books Ltd, Member of BPCC Ltd, Aylesbury, Bucks.